REFLECTIONS ON TH

Liverpool Historical Studies

1. Patrick J. N. Tuck, *French Catholic Missionaries and the Politics of Imperialism in Vietnam, 1857-1914: A Documentary Survey*, 1987, 352pp. (Out of print)
2. Michael de Cossart, *Ida Rubinstein (1885-1960): A Theatrical Life*, 1987, 244pp.
3. P. E. H. Hair, ed., *Coals on Rails, Or the Reason of My Wrighting: The Autobiography of Anthony Errington, a Tyneside colliery waggon and waggonway wright, from his birth in 1778 to around 1825*, 1988, 288pp.
4. Peter Rowlands, *Oliver Lodge and the Liverpool Physical Society*, 1990, 336pp.
5. P. E. H. Hair, ed., *To Defend Your Empire and the Faith: Advice on a Global Strategy Offered c. 1590 to Philip, King of Spain and Portugal, by Manoel de Andrada Castel Blanco*, 1990, 304pp.
6. Christine Hillam, *Brass Plate and Brazen Impudence: Dental Practice in the Provinces 1755–1855*, 1991, 352pp.
7. John Shepherd, *The Crimean Doctors: A History of the British Medical Services in the Crimean War*, 1991, 2 vols, 704pp.
8. John Belchem, ed., *Popular Politics, Riot and Labour: Essays in Liverpool History 1790–1940*, 1992, 272pp.
9. Duncan Crewe, *Yellow Jack and the Worm: British Naval Administration in the West Indies, 1739–1748*, 1993, 352pp.
10. Stephen J. Braidwood, *Black Poor and White Philanthropists: London's Blacks and the Foundation of the Sierra Leone Settlement 1786–1791*, 1994, 336pp.
11. David Dutton, *'His Majesty's Loyal Opposition': The Unionist Party in Opposition 1905–1915*, 1992, 336pp.
12. Cecil H. Clough and P. E. H. Hair, eds, *The European Outthrust and Encounter: The First Phase c.1400–c.1700: Essays in Tribute to David Beers Quinn on His 85th Birthday*, 1994, 380pp.
13. David Dutton, ed., *Statecraft and Diplomacy in the Twentieth Century: Essays Presented to P. M. H. Bell*, 1995, 192pp.
14. Roger Swift, ed., *Victorian Chester, Essays in Social History 1830–1900*, 1996, 263pp.
15. P. E. H. Hair, ed., *Arts · Letters · Society: A Miscellany Commemorating the Centenary of the Faculty of Arts at the University of Liverpool*, 1996, 272pp.
16. Susan George, *Liverpool Park Estates: Their Legal Basis, Creation and Early Management*, 2000, 176pp.
17. Alex Bruce, *The Cathedral 'Open and Free': Dean Bennett of Chester*, 2000, 304pp.
18. David Dutton, *Paris 1918: The War Diary of the British Ambassador, the 17th Earl of Derby*, 2001, 384pp.

REFLECTIONS ON THE BATTLEFIELD

From Infantryman to Chaplain 1914–1919

R.J. Rider

Edited by Alan C. Robinson and P. E. H. Hair

LIVERPOOL UNIVERSITY PRESS

Liverpool Historical Studies, No. 19
General Editor: P. E. H. Hair

Published 2001 by
Liverpool University Press
4 Cambridge Street
Liverpool
L69 7ZU

Text © Miss Elizabeth Rider and Mrs Diana Wass 2001
Introduction and notes © Alan C. Robinson and P. E. H. Hair 2001

All rights reserved. No part of this book may be reproduced, stored in a retrieval system, or transmitted, in any form or by any means, electronic, mechanical, photocopying, recording or otherwise without the prior written permission of the publishers.

British Library Cataloguing-in-Publication Data
A British Library CIP record is available

ISBN 0-85323-887-1 cased
     0-85323-897-9 paperback

Typeset by Northern Phototypesetting Co Ltd, Bolton
Printed in Great Britain by Cromwell Press Ltd, Trowbridge, Wilts.

Dedicated to pals old (1914–1919) and new (1939–1945)

'To err' may be human, but far nobler things are human also.

Contents

	List of Illustrations	viii
	Preface	ix
	Introduction	1
1	Trenches and Mines	38
2	A Minor Wound	45
3	Two Sundays	49
4	In Action	57
5	No-Man's-Land	67
6	Fear Overcome	71
7	Problems of a Padre	75
8	Blood and Fire	82
9	Talking of Death and Censoring Letters	86
10	Gas and Bombs	92
11	A Bad Job	100
12	Prisoners not Enemies	106
13	A German Service	114
14	Victory Hymns	118
15	Horses and Refugees	126
16	Liberation	133
17	Armistice	137
	Epilogue	141
	Index	147

List of Illustrations

The illustrations follow page 70

1. Robert J. Rider in his chaplain's uniform
2. Roclincourt church, pencil drawing by Rider
3. 'Our Home from Home', pencil drawing by Rider
4. Decorating the altar in a church hut
5. Chaplains conducting a memorial service
6. Writing a field postcard for a wounded man
7. Advanced dressing-station, the Somme
8. German POWs carrying stores
9. Collecting the pay books from the dead on the battlefield
10. Ruined buildings, photograph by Rider
11. Army chaplain assisting a refugee
12. Sorting out the packs of the dead and wounded

Preface

We are indebted to the author's surviving relatives for allowing us to publish this text; and especially to Mrs Peggy Rider, his daughter-in-law, who showed us the text after she had typed a transcript, and to Mrs Diana Wass, a grand-daughter, who answered our queries and obtained army records. We thank Terry Carter for supplying information relevant to Rider's infantry career; Dr David Dutton for advice on the military and political aspects of World War I and especially for a constructive reading of the whole manuscript; and Dr Charles Esdaile and Dr Ronald Barr for guidance on the study of army chaplaincy. We acknowledge assistance in tracing records at the Methodist Archive and Research Centre (John Rylands Library, Manchester), the Ministry of Defence (Army Records Centre), and Birmingham University Archives; and also permission for their use. The publishers are grateful to the Imperial War Museum, London, for permission to reproduce the photographs between pages 70 and 71.

Publisher's Note

Sadly, Paul Hair died during the later stages of the production of this book. It is some testimony to a lifetime's devotion to research and scholarship that, critically ill, he completed checking the proofs only days before his death. Paul will be sadly missed by his family and by friends and colleagues around the world.

Introduction

Autobiographical accounts of service in World War I are many, and in relation to the British Army have included a handful documenting the service of chaplains.[1] The present text, while it has limited literary value and adds little to the formal military history of the war on the Western Front, is unique in that its author fought as an infantryman and then served as a chaplain, thus exposing himself, in peculiar directness, to the ambiguities of chaplaincy service on the battlefield. A further particularity is that he was in a minority among army chaplains, being a Methodist chaplain. Since it is unlikely that a document commenting on a similar progress by another individual will now emerge, we must accept the limitations of the present account, including its post-war construction. If its loosely connected anecdotal chapters are insufficiently factual in military detail to be termed in this respect 'history', they are sufficiently factual in testimony to the social and psychological mindset of those involved to be considered more than mere sermons. The historical background to the account is contributed editorially in this introduction and in the notes to the text, but it is not strictly necessary for the reader to digest these to appreciate the sincerity and meaning of the account.

When Robert J. Rider died in 1961, he left to his descendants a typescript text, tentatively entitled 'Flashbacks', which he had abandoned, incomplete, in the early 1950s, apparently after receiving the view of a journalist friend that it was unpublishable. While the extant version seems to have been typed during or immediately after World War II, the form and certain inconsistencies of the text strongly suggest that it was worked on in the 1930s and 1940s, perhaps indeed in the 1920s, and earlier drafts almost certainly drew on a war diary.[2] The text therefore testifies to reflections of two kinds: to battlefield feelings, as the mindset of 1914 was modified by war experiences, and to aspects of the inter-war reaction to the drama of 1914–1918.

Perhaps because it was composed when Rider was an active Christian minister, the account – if it can justly be called that – is broadly autobiographical but takes a peculiar form. It consists of narratives of a number of episodes presented wholly in the third person, based on, but occasionally conflating and even imaginatively expanding, the author's battlefield experiences. Emphasis is laid on the meaning, social and moral, of almost every episode, as understood by Rider and, as far as one dare trust his testimony, by his fellow soldiers.

The author as soldier

In August 1914, Rider, aged twenty-five, was about to begin his third year of training for the ministry of the Wesleyan Methodist church, at Handsworth Theological College in Birmingham.[3] He was not one of the many men who rushed to volunteer within a few days or weeks of Kitchener's recruiting appeal, 'Your King and Country Need You'. But he was among those who enlisted in the immediately following two months; and he joined the First Birmingham Battalion, later termed the 14th Battalion, of the Royal Warwickshire Regiment. The battalion went to France in November 1915 and into the front line in December, moving up again in April to July 1916. During this period Rider served as a signalman and held or attained the rank of Corporal. But in mid-1916 the Wesleyan authorities recalled a number of the men who had been in training for the ministry before joining the army, to serve in future as chaplains in the field, and Rider, returning to England, was commissioned in September 1916. He then ministered to an artillery unit on the Western Front, from January 1917 until the Armistice of November 1918, and he remained in France for some or all of the period up to his eventual demobilisation in late 1919. Even as a chaplain he was at times in the front line of battle and regularly under fire. Hence, in February 1918, he was awarded the Military Cross for 'gallantry and coolness' in rescuing wounded men. Released from the army and resuming his civil vocation, he ministered to various Methodist congregations, especially in Lancashire, but also acted as chaplain to a Territorial Army unit. In World War II he again became a full-time chaplain, but only as an administrator in Britain, never on the battlefield. In 1953 he retired from the ministry.[4]

INTRODUCTION

Pals

In 1957 Rider contributed a small article to the magazine of 'The Old Contemptibles Association'.[5] Rider was not himself one of the 'Old Contemptibles', the nickname adopted to describe the soldiers of the regular army sent to France, as the British Expeditionary Force, on the outbreak of the war, but was instead a 'Pal'.[6] (He dedicated his account to 'Pals old and new, 1914–1919 and 1939–1945'.) In 1914 Britain had no conscription to the military and it became immediately clear that volunteers in large numbers had to be recruited.[7] To encourage men to leave civilian life, Pals battalions were formed, the first in Liverpool, with Birmingham soon following suit. Volunteers shy of coming forward as individuals were persuaded to enlist in groups of workmates or local acquaintances, and, as 'chums' all together, formed into Pals battalions, separate units of the 'New Army'. Men who had worked and played sport together were to fight together – and often die together. As the author of an excellent study of the Birmingham Pals points out, class selection was an additional inducement. Pals had to be decent chaps, defined as 'non-manual workers' – or 'a better class of young men', to quote the *Birmingham Post*. Hence the initial Birmingham Pals tended to be lower middle-class individuals, clerks, librarians, shop assistants, teachers, students, 'the majority church-going, non-swearing teetotallers', literate and often grammar-school educated, but lacking any previous acquaintance with military discipline, culture and mindset.[8]

The First Birmingham Battalion began recruitment in the last days of August and Rider came forward probably several weeks later, in October or November.[9] During the battalion's twelve-month training and equipping in England, Rider was at first in B Company, in Section 8 of Platoon VI. A group photograph taken in July 1915 and an undated but slightly later list show some sixty men in the Platoon.[10] Rider's section of thirteen men contained all six of the students from Handsworth College who had enlisted in the battalion; thus the principle of 'pals' had been so far tightly maintained.[11] But because many of the incoming volunteers to the First Battalion were sooner or later commissioned or otherwise transferred to other regiments, and because companies and sections were reformed to accommodate those with specialist training, it is uncertain whether any of Rider's college colleagues in Section 8 accompanied him into action in France, even at battalion level.[12] However, in 1914 B Company also contained, and seemingly from 1915 to 1917 continued to contain, one

Private J.E.B. Fairclough who, after the war, was to publish in 1933 a useful detailed account of the battalion's military experience, somewhat rigidly conventional, 'written at the salute' and therefore deferential and uncritical, yet with many personal recollections covering the period up to the author's being commissioned and transferred in 1917.[13] It is possible, perhaps likely, that, because of his connection with the battalion and the company, Rider saw this history and was encouraged to pursue his own narrative, with its very different approach and flavour.

The First Birmingham Pals battalion had its earliest casualties, two men of B Company shot by German snipers, shortly after arriving in France and occupying in December 1915 muddy trenches on the Somme. But immediately thereafter casualties were light, when the battalion fought on the Arras section of the front in March–June 1916, and even when back on the Somme in early July. However, two disastrously unsuccessful attacks on Wood Lane in late July led to a slaughter, the battalion sustaining some 600 casualties over eight days. Fairclough was to write that the battalion 'had practically ceased to exist, for so few of the original officers and men were left'.[14] On our count, which is no doubt very incomplete because of transfers, out of the sixty men of Platoon VI photographed in mid-1915, fourteen still serving in the battalion were killed during the war, mostly in July 1916. Section 8 seems to have had only one death, but neighbouring Section 7, of fifteen men, had three – and of these four deaths, three were in July 1916.[15] Of the six college pals in Section 8, one soon disappeared, perhaps commissioned, and none of the others died while in the battalion, but Rider and three others were transferred to become chaplains in August 1916. The restocked Pals battalion suffered another disaster in September 1916, during slightly less unsuccessful attacks on Delville and Leuze Woods, losing 400 men killed and 600 wounded.[16] But by then Rider was no longer with it.

Methodist soldiering

A strand of Wesleyan socio-theological belief was hostile to soldiering. Apart from a distaste for a profession that basically entailed killing other human beings, and a minority pacifist view, Methodists often tended to regard soldiers as particularly unregenerate sinners, wicked in their common use of drink and whores. At one time the denomination discouraged recruiting for the armed forces, and the term 'Wesleyan soldier' was an oxymoron. 'The very application of this honoured term [i.e. Wesleyan] to red-coated drunkards whose very presence in our town is pestilential ... is little less than sacrilege.'[17] However, as the nineteenth century wore on, it became difficult to ignore the presence of a large number of devout Methodists in the army and navy; moreover, as confrontation with the Established Church in England grew in other aspects, the Wesleyan authorities, like their Roman Catholic counterparts at an earlier date, began to fear the proselytising powers of the Church of England (and Church of Scotland), whose chaplains previously held the monopoly of chaplain service. In 1881 a few Wesleyan chaplains were allowed to be appointed.[18] By 1914 a Wesleyan Army and Navy Board existed, although during the war it fretted at the administrative arrangements whereby Wesleyan chaplains served under the umbrella of an Army Chaplains' Department headed by an Anglican Chaplain-General, and were to some extent controlled by the War Office rather than by the church's own power structure.[19]

Whatever their attitude to war in general, most Wesleyans were swept into the flood of patriotic, anti-German and militaristic feeling generated throughout the nation when Belgium was invaded in the first days of August 1914. The righteous war was proclaimed in Britain, and among those responding to a nation-wide outburst of emotion by enlisting were the students of Handsworth Theological College. Thus Rider tells his comrades in France that 'when I enlisted, I earnestly sought a way of establishing righteousness and peace', the latter term being a reference to the view Rider may only later have acquired, that this was 'a war to end wars' (Chapter 3). By November it could be reported by an unhappy correspondent in the *Methodist Times* that, at various colleges, 'certain young men who were being trained for the ministry have relinquished their sacred studies and entered the Army'.[20] The correspondent, apparently a pacifist, called for each and every Christian to dissociate himself from 'this subtle network that drags him at the heels of anti-Christ', the evil defined as 'mere national and imperial aims', and instead seek 'conscious unity with all in other lands who have the great hope and ideal of a united humanity'. A different theological view had been taken in an editorial in the same paper immediately war was declared: 'Now can anyone seriously doubt that our civilisation has merited and needed a purging? Have we [Methodists] meant nothing all these years by our denunciations of godlessness, luxury and frivolity?'[21] The expectation – dangerously convenient and foolishly naive – that a bloody war would 'purge' the nation and produce an uplifted moral order was to haunt Rider in the post-war years and echo dolorously in his account.[22] A few weeks later it was ingeniously argued that there was 'a call to all Christian men who can possibly leave their homes to join the Army, not only to help the nation in a great crisis ... [but also so] that the tone and morale of the Army may be raised'.[23] Perhaps Rider, a bachelor, was influenced by this call. Once Methodist ministerial students had enlisted, a protest followed. A new correspondent argued that they had broken their bond to the church. Furthermore, some might never return, to the loss of the church, yet if they did, 'we may then receive the bread and wine at the Lord's Supper from those hands which have thrust a bayonet through the heart of a fellow-man'.[24] A fortnight later a reply was printed from Private Kingsley East, which while strongly attacking conscientious objectors for sheltering behind soldiers, began by scoring a decisive point. 'I am a Didsbury [Theological College] student now serving in the 7th Manchesters. The correspondence has been unusually interesting to me, as it was introduced by my father. I will not enter into correspondence with my father, but will simply say that my experience so far has shown me that I can do more good in the Army at this time than in the ministry.'[25] Rider's reflections on the moral issues of the war may have developed from these 1914 Methodist debates, but nothing in his account suggests that he regretted enlisting, or felt either any guilt at deserting temporarily his ministry, or, for that matter, any profound relief when ordered to resume it, in another form, as an army chaplain.[26]

Nevertheless, the students of Handsworth College appear to have had mixed feelings about the call to enlist. A report from the college in December 1914 rejoiced that 'the "call of the old Home flag" had not gone unheeded, since even those left in college have not escaped the spirit of the times ... [After compulsory drill] they pace up and down the corridors as though on sentry duty, and have even been known to enter lectures performing the goose-step' [!]. While the number of students in residence at the beginning of the term had been sharply reduced by the onset of the war, against eight who had joined combatant units, six of them the Pals in the First Battalion, eleven had joined the Royal Army Medical Corps and three had been commissioned as army chaplains. This contrasts with the choice of the Methodist students at Cambridge University, most of whom joined combatant units.[27] Nevertheless, it seems that Rider's acceptance of the duty of enlisting for combatant service was not universally the view of the contemporary Methodist student body.

Two years later, Rider's service abruptly changed. As narrated by Fairclough – 'Walking back from Airaines to the camp at Etrejust one party met a group of four [soldiers] walking in the opposite direction. Enquiries were made and the party returning to the battalion was informed, "We are going home to England to become chaplains, you are going back to Delville Wood on Thursday".' Fairclough's anecdote may be thought to embody a probably widespread belief that chaplaincy in the field was a 'cushy' service, hence the alleged words may entirely misrepresent the feelings of Rider and his colleagues.[28] Rider himself wrote as follows:

> That spell in the battle-line ended, and when the unit was out at rest, news came to the Colonel that he [Rider] had been granted a Commission as Chaplain-to-the-Forces. It was with very mixed feelings that he received the news and later said farewell to his old pals, but he was encouraged by the fact that they shared the disappointment with him. As he moved off to the railhead, en route to England, his problem man said: 'Good luck! Try to get back to us, Corporal!' But strong emotion forbade any promise to do so. He did return to the battlefield, but not to his old infantry regiment ...[29]

The number of army chaplains rose during the war from under 120 to over 3,000; the Wesleyan segment rose from a handful to 256.[30] At first, the dramatic growth of the army was not matched by the recruitment of chaplains, and the troops' suspicions regarding chaplaincy service – especially Anglican – were related to the fact that chaplains were inevitably seldom encountered, other than on rare official occasions, and then in some instances in localities not close to the fighting action.[31] But by 1916, the various church authorities were acting to provide many more chaplains, and the Wesleyans, who since 1914 had mainly sought chaplains by requesting circuits to release their minister, a limited strategy, now agreed that 'to prevent further dislocation of circuit work, appointments should, as far as possible, be made from ministers serving in the army'.[32] Rightly or wrongly, the reference to 'ministers serving in the army' was taken to mean, more logically, 'ministerial students serving in the army', and hence the recall of Rider.[33] It is not clear what additional training or pastoral experience, if any, he was given – by the church and/or the army – between his appointment as a chaplain on 1 September 1916 and his embarking for France on 11 January 1917.[34] The impression his account gives is that he was unexpectedly recalled and obeyed his church's orders, but was then thrown into army chaplaincy with little guidance provided and had to 'learn on the job'.[35] Another impression his text gives is that he did not, indeed could not, limit his chaplain's duties to ministering to Methodists, whatever those at home had intended.

Battles of an infantryman and chaplain

Only the first six chapters, out of the present edition of eighteen, refer to Rider's time as an infantryman.[36] Other accounts indicate that the enthusiastic young men of Birmingham and district, 'of a better class', who left Birmingham in October 1914 – in trains with cheery chalked messages such as 'Berlin via Sutton'— at times found difficulty in adjusting to the vicissitudes of camp life during their training and equipping in England.[37] The length of their training was partly due to the late arrival of uniforms and weapons, rifles being issued to them only six weeks before they left for France.[38] Rider, however, seems to have been selected at an early stage for specialist training, as a signalman, and his account makes it clear that he served as a signalman throughout his time as an infantryman in France.[39] Their work made signalmen more flexible than their infantry companions in respect of attachment to specific units within the battalion, and it is likely that Rider was permanently detached from B Company.[40] The battalion sailed to France on 21 December 1915, and immediately had to undertake a series of arduous and sometimes unnecessary route marches, from the coast to the Somme. At the first stage 300 men fell out, to the colonel's disgust, and we have considered whether an episode described by Rider, now forming Chapter 2 of his account, did not occur on this occasion.[41] But the light-heartedness of the yarn (which Rider inserted as 'a separate story' and which perhaps originally formed part of another manuscript) barely fits the mood of the 1915 event, the battalion's introduction to hard slog, and the episode is more likely to have occurred on a later march. The earliest battle episodes are those described in Chapter 1 – the chapter includes references to a signaller and concludes with the unnamed narrator described as 'the Corporal'. These episodes relate to the Arras front, in Spring 1916, Rider having passed over without mention the battalion's muddy but almost bloodless few weeks on the Somme.[42] A devastating explosion of a German mine under the front-line position of the 15th Warwickshires, followed by a trench raid by the Germans, is noted, a little problematically; it occurred on 4 June 1916.[43] The 14th battalion was in the trenches immediately to the left, near the village of Roclincourt, 'a typical ruined one' according to Fairclough, and Rider produced two pen-and-ink drawings of destruction in the village.[44] In the Epilogue to his account, Rider recollected that 'most [French] villages had, at both entries, the sacred figure of the Crucifix'; one of his Roclincourt drawings shows a battered crucifix among the ruins of what appears to have been a churchyard, and the historian of the battalion noted that 'above the signallers' dugout was the Calvary of the village'.[45]

Between the Somme and the Arras experiences, the battalion had an unexpectedly extended rest period, an outbreak of German measles putting it in quarantine for two months, January–March 1916.[46] Rider dwells on this period (Chapter 3) as one in which he obtained opinions about the war and, revealing his background, began quasi-chaplain activities.[47] In June–July 1916 the battalion was back on the Somme, and Rider's Chapters 4–6 cover the two unsuccessful and deadly attacks in later July which decimated – Fairclough's term – the battalion. The narrator is now 'Corporal J. in the Signals Section' (Chapter 5) and 'the Signals Corporal' (Chapter 6).[48] The theme of these chapters is bravery and bloodshed, but Rider does not comment on the military mistakes, his interest being in small-scale episodes which illuminate human character and, as he saw it, God's providential mercy.

In August 1916 Rider left the battalion and in January 1917 returned to France as a chaplain. He was attached to an artillery unit, apparently for most of his remaining wartime service, but his account is now even more frugal regarding the specifics of his army career, and we have been unable to identify the artillery regiment. Appropriate to the horse-drawn artillery of the time, the account begins to contain frequent references to horses, and at one point Rider seems to forget his new non-combatant role by guiding the movement of horsed waggons carrying supplies to the guns (Chapter 10). In Spring 1917 the regiment was in the Arras section and Rider refers to the attack from that town beginning on Easter Monday (9 April 1917), whose gains included Vimy Ridge (Chapter 11).[49] The regiment must have then moved north since he refers to the 'Battle of Ypres' later that year (Chapters 10–13). A black South African soldier, dying slowly and bravely, becomes the subject of an anecdote (Chapter 14); while the rout of the Portuguese division during the German offensive of April 1918 is mentioned (Chapter 15).[50] As a chaplain, and as one serving with the artillery, Rider was now less frequently in the front-line trenches, yet perhaps as frequently under fire from shells and air attack.[51] In June 1918 Rider was awarded the Military Cross for rescuing wounded men under fire, at Poelkapelle on the Ypres front; his account narrates several similar exploits by others but omits mention of his own act.[52] The end of the war was approaching. Rider consorts with German prisoners (Chapters 13–14) and when acting as billeting officer for the advancing British troops (apparently regarded as an appropriate non-combatant duty) comes upon German wounded (Chapter 16).[53] In these final months of warfare, as part of a larger responsibility, he seems to have gone forward at times with the infantry.[54] The Armistice of November 1918 arrives when Rider's unit is within ten miles of Mons, but Rider agrees with the view of the 'Tommies' that the defeated Germans should have been pursued to Berlin (Chapter 17). The aftermath of the war takes a curious form in Rider's experience, for 1919 sees him ministering to soldiers in a French hospital which now specialises in those casualties of war prevented from early return to Britain by the damage, not of shot and shell, but of venereal diseases (Epilogue).[55]

Chaplaincy

The tasks of a chaplain were multifarious, although not all were mandatory. When appropriate and convenient, he took regular church services, whether official church parades or less formal worship. He took burial services or committals, when corpses were recovered (on the battlefield many men dissolved in fragments or totally disappeared, declared 'missing'). He organised mild recreations – but also helped to censor letters. On a reclaimed battlefield he, with others, identified corpses, by seeking and collecting the tags and papers on the bodies, and he might keep a record of the identities and burial place, and return the most precious personal possessions to a dead man's family.[56] During a battle he might also collect messages from the wounded, to notify their families.[57] Finally, he assisted in minor ways the other non-combatants, the medical services, while ministering to the wounded and sick.[58]

Rider refers to most of these activities. When the war ended he regretted that the 'restored parade service', that is, a weekly church parade, was 'dwarfing, if not actually spoiling the ministries of consolation and help' (Chapter 17).[59] He notes services of formal worship at a hospital (Chapter 13), but describes only informal services: one in a trench, another in 'a large hole' accommodating only twenty men – or fewer officers (Chapter 7). His separate service for officers came to an abrupt and bloody end, but later he establishes and conducts, on three Sundays, a service for German prisoners (Chapter 13). In between, the account notes that 'the unofficial side of the Chaplain's work was the limit of his activities for some time' (Chapter 7) – but the term 'unofficial' surely misrepresents the activities in which, putting church services on one side, he is thereafter constantly engaged. He searches the battlefield and collects the identifying belongings of the dead, and he brings a burial party to the remains, or directs the

INTRODUCTION

burial of a sudden casualty (Chapters 11, 14). Afterwards, 'the Padre was sitting by the light of smoking candles, writing. Thirty letters, with almost as many packages of personal effects found on the bodies of the fallen – photographs, letters, cuttings, and many other things including simple "charms" – [were] all to be despatched to the homes of the next-of-kin to which the loved one would never return' (Chapter 14). Out of the line, the task of the Padre with a battalion (Rider explains) was to be 'largely responsible for filling in the hours of the men with sit-around talks and arguments' – what the men called a 'pow-wow' and apparently indulged in even when no chaplain was encouraging them (Chapter 3). No doubt, however, other modes of recreation, some organised by chaplains and some certainly not, were for many soldiers more popular. After the war ended, in order 'to counteract the dangers of an idle mind and idle hands', chaplains were expected to provide 'varied and interesting pastimes', which might include 'talks and lectures' intended to aid the return to civilian life (Epilogue). As Rider hints, the 'dangers' were principally the seeking out of those in a later war aptly termed 'comfort women', but inevitably, during the rest and local leave periods of war, the *estaminet* (Chapter 3) and the related services of Mademoiselle from Armentières had been widely welcomed. Yet letters were written to wives and sweethearts, and the Padre, required to censor these – reading them being, as Rider wryly notes, 'part of the Padre's education' – found a way of respecting the privacy of some correspondents by acting as confidential postman (presumably against army regulations) (Chapter 9).

Back on the battlefield, the chaplain gave first aid to those lightly wounded and helped at dressing-stations, on one occasion leading in 'a blinded man and a lamed man, one on each arm' (Chapter 14); he accompanied stretcher-bearers and organised the collective conveyance of wounded men (Chapters 10, 12); he carried to a safe place a dying officer (Chapter 11); and, as part of the 'ministry of consolation', in the form of addressing, on the battlefield and later, the desperately wounded and dying, he was at one point attached to a hospital (Chapter 13). Apart from these duties, mandatory or self-imposed, Rider valued the occasional opportunity to chat with others, perhaps not so much with the officer colleagues of his new rank as with the ordinary soldiers representing the comrades of his infantry experience, talking to them and even listening to them. From the officers' mess he sought out the gun line and horse lines, and when another Padre went sick and passed on his duties Rider was glad 'to renew his acquaintance with the trenches', that is, with infantry (Chapter 7). As a chaplain, he 'missed his old pals and their chumminess which had meant so much to him' (Chapter 7). The dialogues of the account suggest that Rider believed that, even as a chaplain, he could talk simply 'man to man'; whether those who called him 'Sir' thought quite the same must be open to a measure of doubt. The account is silent as to the extent to which, in these casual conversations, Rider pressed specific God-talk.

Although Rider moved from infantryman to chaplain, and found the transformation in some aspects traumatic, there was no abrupt switch in his moral interests. As an infantryman, he found himself in early 1916 organising church services on two Sundays (Chapter 3). Then, as the corporal of a digging party attempting to rescue men buried when a mine explodes, he calls the other members to attention and gives 'a few simple words of an improvised committal' (Chapter 1). Over a dying officer in no-man's-land, the corporal breathes silently, 'Into Thy hands, O God' (Chapter 5). During an attack he encourages a signaller who has emotionally collapsed (and shields him from being shot for cowardice) by assuring him that God will give him strength to recover and continue (Chapter 6). The account avers that, when Rider eventually became a chaplain, 'a report had already been made on his voluntary work' (Chapter 7), which presumably means that the army reported on his quasi-chaplain activities. Throughout his infantry service, Rider contemplates the moral issues of warfare, the narrative occasionally depicting the issues as having been raised by the ordinary soldiers, his comrades.

Attitudes

It is difficult for personal narratives about the 'Great War' to be other than didactic; Rider's account is morally, even theologically, didactic, and deliberately so. He wished to convey to others the moral lessons he had learned – or perhaps to some extent re-learned – during the war. In simple summary, these derived from an interplay between two ideals, his Christian beliefs and his experience of 'comradeship' with 'pals' and 'chums'. They are most explicitly stated in the final chapter of his text. Men (that is, humankind, although there are hardly any women in Rider's account) are not, as the Prophet Jeremiah would have it, 'deceitful above all things and desperately wicked' – or at least, not merely so, for in certain circumstances they exhibit 'comradeship, sacrifice and service'. The circumstances that had proved this to him were 'the communal life of Army days', and therefore the war. The evil of the war had, after all, by God's merciful dispensation, produced good, not just because it was a righteous war (and therefore to be won by the Allies, although Rider makes almost no flag-waving assent to the general point), but because 'God has a wonderful way of rescuing men from what would harm them, using the very harms themselves to serve a nobler purpose'. Hence, in the vast majority of cases, 'men learned more about the heights to which humanity can rise than about the depths to which it could sink' (Epilogue). While there was a Panglossian flavour to this optimistic viewpoint, yet it was surely not altogether an illusion that many British soldiers displayed in battle, not merely a gritty stoicism, but on occasions a degree of un-self-regarding devotion to comrades.[60]

Rider's admiration for his comrades was well-nigh unbounded and is exemplified in anecdote after anecdote. He commends their 'inexhaustible wit' (Chapter 1) and the 'quiet manner in which comrades act when faced with danger' (Chapter 4); but also recognises the 'strange cheerfulness that accompanies acknowledged defeat' (Chapter 1). Although the period of 'dull monotony of stagnant warfare' was distressing, nevertheless more active battle was 'void of any attractiveness', yet the British soldiers faced up to 'another dose of unquestioned duty' (Chapter 6). Their 'new stoicism', 'their spirit of apparent unconcern', was set against the realisation that they had 'experienced failure and learnt what it cost in human sacrifice' (Chapter 1). This was their 'heroic forgetfulness' (Chapter 2). Their courage could be more than mere bravado: 'One should not look for bravery in callous men. It is seen in men who first knew fear' (Chapter 6).

It is plausible that, inasmuch as Rider was one of the 'better sort' recruited as Pals in 1914, previously he had been little acquainted with the ranks of those less well educated and more down-market. Yet, as the war wound on, he seems to have found it instructive and even exhilarating to meet and mix with those of a different background. The dialogues he presents, albeit to some extent contrived and stereotyped, are frequently presented as involving individuals whose speech is, in accent and content, less sophisticated than his own. But these are also the men 'willing, at any cost, to answer a call of need; men who had practised unselfishness in times both of want and plenty; men who had been courageous in battle, heroic in pain, calm in dangers that regularly threatened their lives; men who had learned to recognise the voice of God in their sense of duty to one another and who had shown wonderful readiness to obey it; men who knew their fellows, even their enemies, well enough to be able to love them, and to hate the means whereby fellow men had been exterminated'

(Epilogue). The Church should welcome the privilege of the co-operation of such men. Although there was a degree of understandable professional bias in the claim that attachment to duty derived from religious recognition, Rider's deeply sincere belief in regenerate humanity is patent.

Despite the friendship and comradeship, Rider noted that service in the ranks had 'killed initiative in action and originality of thought' (Chapter 7). However, the positive aspect persisted; he summed up his later role in an attractive if somewhat superficial phrase – 'chaplaincy in the field is really comradeship' (Chapter 7). He justly commented that the role of an army chaplain (and perhaps particularly that of a Nonconformist chaplain with a temporary wartime commission) was less than secure in the military pecking order; 'it was difficult to decide whether a Padre was part of the Army or only attached to it – whether with honorary rank he was really an officer, or just shown the courtesies of rank by fellow members of the mess' (Chapter 7). Nevertheless he clearly enjoyed his new spiritual command (and he had, after all, been in voluntary training for this vocation before the war). His appreciation of his new colleagues was a shade lush, a 'jolly good lot' (Chapter 9), but perhaps only adjectivally different from his view of his former colleagues. He gives a charitable interpretation to the officers gossiping about the men they command (Chapter 8). He momentarily takes aboard the military ideal when he speaks of 'the honour of the Battery' (Chapter 9). His entertaining dialogues with choleric colonels are almost music-hall, whereas his closer sympathies seem to lie with the younger officers. These he is soon addressing, and to some extent talking down to, as a senior old hand.

Possibly Rider's Nonconformist heritage of 'man to man' helped in his relations with both men and officers.[61] His passing references to church parades fall under the Nonconformist condemnation of 'official religion', and he refers disparagingly to 'official burial in the tombs of a cathedral' (Chapter 1) – 'official' being a Nonconformist code-word for the established churches. Perhaps his avowed desire 'to translate Christian theories into practical ministries' (Chapter 14) smacks a little of the Social Gospel which by the 1900s had heavily influenced Nonconformity. However, although he does not comment on the established churches of Britain, in the Epilogue he admits to having been impressed by the outward signs of the Roman Catholic devotion of the battlefield villages, and he emits gasps of ecumenicism (Epilogue).[62] On balance, it cannot be said that his Nonconformity is intrusive, certainly as weighed against the pervasiveness of his overall religious and Christian beliefs. Among the Pals of lower middle-class Birmingham background, Rider's beliefs and religious practices would not have stood out, but the changing social set-up of the battalion by 1916 is indicated in the episode of his elevation by his comrades to spiritual leader. Just as a colonel reflected upper-crust limits to religious involvement in his view that a service of worship would be 'a bit of a change for the men' (Chapter 3),[63] so the strand of working-class 'neutrality' regarding religion, or at least confessional religion, appears in the dialogue. Rider is challenged: 'It must be blooming hard work trying to preach religion these days. There's no place for the sob stuff is there?' The men, who have 'managed so far' without a service, are amused to plan for their corporal 'a nightshirt' (i.e., a surplice) and a pulpit (Chapter 3).[64] Rider now proceeds on his path towards a chaplaincy, but he tells us little about his previous Christian activity. Since he approves of a Salvation Army adherent who influences a sinner by kindness, 'yet never said a word to him in the old way about religion' (Chapter 8), we may speculate that Rider did not himself practise evangelistic button-holing. But he may well have been visible to others, even in the front line, when at private prayers and Bible-reading.

Rider's search for the positive in his experience, partly as an expression of his religious faith, limits his explicit negative judgement of events.[65] He served 'five interminable years' (Epilogue), noting that among 'the rotten effects of war' was that 'one gets accustomed to degrading and cruel things' (Chapter 9). As noted above, in what is most likely a post-war reflection he claims that his comrades 'hated the means whereby fellow men had been exterminated' (Epilogue). But he does not dwell on the moral indecencies. Although he deals sympathetically with the chaplain's duty of censoring letters (Chapter 9), he makes relatively little of the soldiers' separation from their families – the 'home life and family associations for which men had risked their lives' (Epilogue) – except in the curious and incomplete anecdote in Chapter 10 where Jim's parents worry about him almost as much when he is on leave as when on the battlefield.[66] But this blind spot is probably because as a chaplain he is most conscious, and indeed deeply conscious, of the family aspect when he has to communicate with bereaved relatives (Chapter 14). He does dwell on the sufferings of wounded men, but with almost as much emphasis on the mental trauma – their fear and isolation – as on the physical. Overarching his approach to the slaughter he witnessed, but nowhere directly addressed, is his attitude to death. At a commonplace level death is 'a deep and peaceful sleep' (Chapter 5), wiping out the pains of human existence. But at a Christian level it is an entrance to God's glory in the 'Great

Beyond' (Chapter 6). Somehow, in a way not fully revealed to humankind, the dead soldier is rewarded for his dutifulness and courage – Rider does not consider the issue of the enemy soldier,[67] or the unheroic warrior. The battlefield dead would 'give an account of what they had done in the "Great War" to Him whose recognition of service is more generous and unerring' (Chapter 5).[68] Some battlefield corpses, he claims, have a smile on their faces, smiles that 'gave one the impression that they had heard the "Well done!" that makes everything worthwhile'. And he does not hesitate to use a phrase of mysticism – the dying soldier is 'enjoying death' (Chapter 14). This particular solution to battlefield experience – anathema to the humanist writers who emerged – was of course not original but traditional, and perhaps more universal than essentially Christian. An emotional solution, at times sentimental to a fault, it nevertheless met a genuine and not easily dismissed psychological need. It was certainly closer to the mindset and sentiments of many of the practising soldiery of the time than the later view that they were mere passive or unthinking victims, wickedly tricked into wasting their lives. Probably a majority of them knew, at the very least, the implied promise of the well-known (because brief) Psalm 23: 'Yea, though I walk through the valley of the shadow of death, I will fear no evil: for thou art with me ... and I will dwell in the house of the Lord for ever.'

When challenged that there was no room for preaching religion these days, 'especially out here', Rider responded, feebly and somewhat pathetically, 'It's not quite that bad surely. There is a bit of religion out here, don't you think?' (Chapter 3). A German prisoner is made to inquire, much to the point, 'We would like to know where God comes in, in this war' (Chapter 13). Rider's response was simple, for intellectual sceptics over-simple. His account was designed to show that the war was 'not quite that bad' and, like other seemingly catastrophic situations, could be redeemed by religious belief.[69] In the language of Victorian tradition (but not Rider's words), it was possible to 'improve the occasion' by relating it to the workings of divine providence. The tenable overall belief in divine providence is, however, all too frequently sabotaged by linking it to the capacity of the human commentator to explain the detailed workings of providence, that is, generally, to explain them away; and Rider fell into this trap. His attempt to quibble – 'This tragedy was perhaps not staged by providence, but can be used by Providence' – was perfunctorily and justly dismissed by his colonel (Chapter 7); but Rider continued to think of the war as an 'opportunity' for individual moral gain, a sort of test laid down by divine providence. (Ultimately, of course, this is the dilemma of free will, which has intrigued and baffled sharper minds than Rider's.)[70] Less worthy, perhaps, was his strong hint that he himself had been spared by providence: 'A dozen times at least I have been missed by inches. ... I don't believe it's all luck'. However, he instantly side-stepped full conviction, by adding, for the benefit of his secular listener, 'You'd expect me to say that, I suppose' (Chapter 9).

Finally, inasmuch as the account is a historical discourse, what can be deduced from it about the attitudes of the common soldiery, Rider's comrades on the battlefield and in the trenches? Undeniably, allowance must be made for the literary transmission, and the dialogues are particularly suspect. He cannot have remembered the statements which are presented as if verbatim. Their wrapping up in dialect of a sort, working-class argot, as contemporaneously conceived by the generality of writers, does not help.[71] Occasionally he can be accused of writing down his comrades, as when he repeats their naïve remarks and incidentally demonstrates his own intellectual superiority, patronisingly.[72] Yet, to the editors, the general thrust of his record of attitudes, given certain reservations, rings true – although it is likely that not all historians will agree. Later generations, and perhaps Rider himself when writing up his recollections, have, however, been 'brainwashed' by a view of World War I which, despite much revisionist writing, persists in the popular mind.

A well-disseminated critique of the British Army on the Western Front is summed up in the catchy phrase, 'lions led by donkeys'. Rider was a colleague of both the lions and the donkeys. The acclaimed War Poets, especially Owen and Sassoon, originated this line of rhetoric, although it has been heightened by the anti-Establishment cult of the later twentieth century.[73] Anti-war literature found easy targets for bitter anger and deeply-felt pity – but excesses of both can slip into the self-congratulatory location of the high moral ground. The ultimate targets were the 'Victorian values' of religion and patriotism. Rider could not possibly share these targets, any more than the poets' dismissal of those at home as hypocrites and smug betrayers of the men dying on the battlefield. Sassoon excoriated a hypothetical bishop safely at home for too smoothly commending divine providence, by parroting the words, 'The ways of God are strange'; Rider also commended divine providence – and in fact shared with the bishop a too-convenient religious expectation about the outcome of the war[74] – but he generated his commendation from personal experience of the battlefield.

Further, it has been argued that the compassion of the War Poets, albeit genuine, was somewhat lofty, the poets being themselves members of the officer class; and that it could be even patronising, when they pitied the dependent soldiery as passive 'cattle'.[75] Rider's colleagues, whether infantry in the trenches or officers encountered when a chaplain, are intrinsically more human. His infantry are variegated and vocal 'cattle', with self-regarding minds and reactive reflections— even if latter-day generations cannot bring themselves to comprehend mindsets which hallowed social deference and heroic patriotism[76] – so that Rider allows shadier characters, and contradictory characteristics, among his lions. And he does not dissociate the officers from the lions – although it is true that his personal encounters approach the 'donkeys' of the High Command no nearer than a couple of colonels, a brigade commander, and two staff officers.[77] The passion of the poets, their war rage, has been justly admired.[78] Rider exhibits a passion too, one humbler, non-literary, more diffused, one not devoid of an idealistic cast and therefore subject to the temptation of loftiness, yet one more broadly empathetic – and conceivably more true to the facts.

Nevertheless, one long passage in Chapter 3 of Rider's account, representing a conversation between Rider and a group of infantrymen, is both puzzling and problematic. In our view the several dialogues cannot wholly have taken place at the time indicated.[79] But they may still represent, in part, honestly recollected segments of discourse containing elements approximating to what was said to Rider by various soldiers, even though at points they appear to be coloured by his post-war reflections. The conversation is rambling and composed of loosely related sets of remarks thrown out confusingly by a handful of speakers, without any final conclusion. But several directions of thrust, all comments on the war, can be distinguished.

The first is a complaint that the war as conducted is not sporting enough, because the combatants do not meet but simply hurl explosives at each other; 'What scope is there out here for showing what kind of a soldier you are?' Moreover, such distance-combat has led to stalemate: 'I can't see how we are going to get much forrader carrying on like this'. This wholly plausible but superficial complaint about strategy leads on to a more thoughtful comment, although it involves a complaint which contradicts the previous one about the dominance of distance-combat, a complaint that killing a man in face-to-face fighting is disgusting: 'Why should I have to stick this [bayonet] into any man ... ?'[80] But since, ineluctably, warfare means killing, can war be justified? While this was no doubt one of Rider's own major ethical problems, the conversation avoids the general principle and instead questions why Germans have to be killed. 'I've no grudge against any Fritz. I don't know any of them, and I don't see how any of them can have a grudge against me as none of them knows me.' This again is a plausible, because small-minded, comment. The speaker continues by noting that 'some of them are decent enough fellows' – but this sounds like Rider drawing on his own experience with German prisoners, as later related, and probably also reflecting his interwar desire for reconciliation. A final objection to the conduct of the war is that it necessitates hate and inhumane behaviour. 'It's when we get these damned rifles in our hands that by now our fingers glide instinctively to the trigger, and our eyes scan the horizon, almost in the hope that we can see a Boche to have a go at … When I drop it at the end of this show, I'll wash my hands of its pollution.' Again, 'We don't often get parsons here telling us chaps what we ought to do to be a decent fellow, 'cause the next minute we get an officer coming and telling us to go over the top, and that means acting like a b… beast'. This final moral objection, and particularly its reference to 'pollution', is surely Rider preaching, although it is plausible (we suggest) that a soldier did point out the contrast between parsons and officers, not to underline the immorality of the latter but the impracticality of the former.

It is equally difficult to be sure to what extent we are hearing the voice of the common soldier in the part of the discussion about the motive for the war. A soldier speaks out: 'I'd like to know whose b… scrap it is. It ain't mine.' And again, 'When you starts a thinkin' like, you wonder what yer doin' in this show at all'. Rider claims that, as their corporal, he distracted the men from 'conversation running in a dangerous channel', being confident that allowing them 'to "let off steam" would not affect their loyalty'. But his own contribution was in part no less subversive, if not entirely logical. 'There's something wrong with things when, though we don't like having to do it, we cannot help being involved in a war like this.' This particular comment is capable of being interpreted as no more than repeating a 1914 Methodist view of the conflict, that it was the necessary purging of an already wicked world. However, Rider continues: 'When I enlisted, I earnestly sought a way of establishing righteousness and peace. To me a sword or a bayonet seemed very unworthy instruments in such a noble enterprise. I would have used anything else that could have been found to do this, but I searched in vain. It's not that I am a coward but I don't like the business and I don't think we are hitting the right man when we strike.' Remembering that Rider had opted in 1914 for combatant service, rather than the non-combatant service chosen by some of his fellow students, this comment comes close to trying to have it both ways. But he exculpates himself by concluding that 'I'm here because I've been persuaded that this is to be the last of wars.' The account then adds a curious sentence: '"A war to end war" came from a gentlemanly fellow who had been following the discussion with almost disturbing keenness.' That the 1914–1918 war was the 'war to end wars' was certainly a much-repeated slogan of the inter-war decades. The curiously specific sentence (since the 'gentlemanly fellow' is neither explained nor followed up) almost, but not quite, convinces us that this part of the conversation is historical and that Corporal Rider actually spoke in these terms in 1916. One further complaint remains. The remark about the 'scrap' not being that of the ordinary soldiery and the author's thought that 'the right man' was not being struck, seem, at first glance, to echo the contemporary view of international socialism and a section of the British Labour Party, to the effect that the war was the result of a conspiracy of international capitalists. It is certainly not implausible that among those taking part in the pow-wow (or among those elsewhere and later encountered by Rider) were soldiers who held and would utter this view. But it may instead be that Rider, in both comments, or perhaps at least in his own, was expressing the form of political quasi-pacificism which in the inter-war decades laid the blame for wars on international arms-dealers.[81] A simpler explanation of his own remark about 'not the right man' is nevertheless available. He was merely putting the blame for the war on the Kaiser, albeit perhaps as the figurehead of incompetent international statesmanship, and was thus repeating a popular contemporary British view, one which he may well have actually held and stated in 1916, and above all one which allowed him to consider, then or later, German soldiers as not the real enemy.

This passage has been examined in detail because it is different in tone from the rest of the account. Nowhere else is the patriotic war explicitly challenged. We do not claim to understand why this outburst of examination of the ethics of the battlefield occurs in this fashion and at this point within the text. Undoubtedly, whatever its antecedents in factual history, it largely represents Rider's own moral concerns, and perhaps to some extent his developing post-war ones. We have suggested that it may have been influenced by current post-1918 intellectual fashions. Yet it differs considerably from the point of view of the War Poets and their disciples. We have pointed out above that the account as a whole presents a more variegated and therefore more positive assessment of the British soldiery. But further, this passage in critique of the war, while it resembles the poetry in dissociating itself from the triumph of killing enemy individuals, includes not a word of pity for the numbers slaughtered or the physical sufferings, not even those on the British side. Rider's soldiers lack self-pity.

We conclude that Rider's account, with its central assertion of belief in 'the universal need for, and practice of, comradeship' (Chapter 7), offers a small but significant contribution to the present-day debate about the contemporary understanding of the ethics of war, as expressed on the World War I battlefield.

APPENDIX

Date of composition of the text

Although the dedication refers to '1939–1945', the last paragraph of the final chapter contains a reference to World War II as still in progress. Apart from this paragraph, this 'Epilogue' chapter, with its sad complaint about the loss of Christian fellowship after 1918, and the deficiencies of the Church, seems to reflect in mood Rider's experiences in the 1920s and 1930s as a circuit minister, and is therefore perhaps less likely to have been originally composed in 1939–1945 when he was again a full-time army chaplain. Again, his references in Chapter 14 to German prisoners anxious to attend church services and to his friendly response, and in general his failure to condemn German actions as evil, suggest that he was writing during the inter-war decades of 'reconciliation', rather than during World War II, when British attitudes to Germans hardened, to say the least. Finally, the chapter of the typescript presented as Chapter 2 of the present edition has added to it in ink not only the statement that this is 'An extra story not included in the MS', but also an address for Rider, at Tyldesley, in the Leigh circuit which he served in the 1930s. This appears to confirm the suggestion that writing of some sort preceded World War II. The existence of a war diary (rather than surviving battlefield letters sent home which most likely would have been less specific) is indicated by the quotations from soldier's letters censored by Rider (Chapter 9), quotations which can have been noted only at the time. That Rider brought back and retained certain material composed on the battlefield is indicated by the drawings of Roclincourt, one of which is dated '1916'.

Style and editing of the text

Rider chose to supply few factual details of place and date. The only places named in the text are Arras (Chapter 11), Ypres ('Battle of Ypres', Chapter 13), and Mons (Chapter 17). One of the two drawings by Rider, almost certainly both made at the time (1916), is captioned 'Rocklingcourt church', the place being Roclincourt, a village two miles north of Arras. In the text dates are only once given, and that only the date of the Armistice of November 1918, although there are allusions to the passing of time. References in Chapters 2 and 6 to two years' 'foot-slogging', and in Chapter 10 to two-and-a-half years since a German advance in Belgium, may be noted. There is some evidence that in the course of the various recensions and rearrangements made by the author, the strict chronology of events was disregarded or overlooked. The narratives are now mostly arranged in approximate chronological order, as justified in the editorial apparatus, but here and there some overlap may be suspected.

Rider also chose to write in the third person, and he intended the text, if published, to be pseudonymous.[82] The closest to his own naming occurs in the somewhat out-of-place Chapter 2 where the hero is 'Bob', no doubt Robert Rider's appellation among his family and comrades. Elsewhere the account refers only to 'the Corporal', 'the Signals Corporal' and 'the Padre', apart from a single reference by an officer to 'Corporal J.' (Chapter 5) – although Rider's middle name was John, it is difficult to understand this excessive concealment, unless he was known to officers, not as 'Bob', but as 'John'. The account is equally discreet about the names of others; the men are only 'Bill', 'Jock', 'Sam', 'Tom' and 'Jim', or are nicknamed 'Badger' and 'Fiz' (with a German being 'Fritz'), and an NCO is only 'Corporal T...'. Among the officers, only 'Woods', 'Potts' and 'old Byron' are given a surname, a dying officer being only 'Lieutenant H...', while 'Mac', presumably a nickname, suffices for not one but two artillery officers.

The view of the friend that the text could not be published, at least as it stood, is understandable. Rider left the material in some confusion. The typescript, typed by the author himself, badly, has erasions and additions in ink and pencil, and consists of chapters from two recensions. One set has chapters numbered 6–30, with gaps, on pages numbered 15–123; another set has chapters numbered 14–16 and 20, on pages 158–206. The pages of illustrations Rider prepared ('Close-ups through the Battle Smoke') were noted to appear opposite pages 88, 117, 191 and 203. A possible explanation of these references to a text of over 200 pages is that they referred to a manuscript which preceded the extant typescripts. The two forms of Chapters 15, 16 and 20 differ totally in content. Throughout, pages were often renumbered. Obviously revision was never completed and some initial chapters, presumably dealing with the first eighteen months of army service, seem to have been lost. The original of Chapter 2 of this present edition has written on it, 'An extra short story not included in the MS'. At points where the recensions create confusion in the progress of the narrative, editorial decisions as to which version to follow have been made. The general content of the text is, however, unchanged, and the order of the larger set has been generally followed. Other editorial contributions have been as follows. Paragraphs and chapters that are too brief have been run together when this makes narrative sense. Chapters are untitled in the typescript but a number have suggested titles added in ink or pencil. Because of our running together of chapters, most chapter titles have been editorially supplied, as has the title for the whole account. In copy-editing, attention has been paid to the punctuation, a few slips corrected, confused syntax sorted out, and occasional stylistic infelicities amended. Finally, an article published anonymously in the November 1957 issue of *The Old Contemptible* but not represented in the typescript has been inserted as Chapter Seventeen.

Notes

1 The most recent are Jonathan Horne, ed., *The Best of Good Fellows: The Diaries and Memoirs of the Rev. Charles Edmund Doundney, M.A., C.F.* [killed in action October 1915], London, 1995; John Bickersteth, ed., *The Bickersteth Diaries 1914–1918*, London, 1995 (with an introduction by John Terraine). The latter work supplies extracts from copious letters written from the battlefield by two brothers, Julian, a Church of England chaplain serving in France from February 1916, and Burgon, a cavalry officer, who had previously worked for a time as a 'lay missionary'; a third brother, also serving in France, was killed on 1 July 1916. In background the two brothers differed in most respects from the author of the present account. Scions of a well-placed Establishment clerical dynasty, therefore upper middle class, public school and Oxbridge, with contacts in high places, including academia, they were highly literate, multilingual, vocal and articulate. Julian was a volunteer chaplain, with pre-war pastoral experience (as was Doundney). Despite the differences, and the superior historical quality of the Bickersteths' contemporary letters (whereas there are no Rider family letters), resemblances between the experiences of the two chaplains frequently occur. For purposes of confirmation, comparison, or contrast, or to fill out slight comments in the account, references to the Bickersteth letters are given below, the work hereafter cited, according to the individual writer, as '*Bickersteth* JB' or '*Bickersteth* BB'. (The work is entitled

'Diaries' because the letters were copied in a typescript 'diary' kept by the brothers' mother; and since only extracts from the letters have been to date published, it should be noted that two levels of editorial selection apply.) Although Rider and Bickersteth were both chaplains and at times served on the same section of the front, and although the Anglican one has a few references to Wesleyan padres, it is unlikely that the two ever met.

2 The friend's opinion was given in 1952, in a letter tactfully stating that the typescript he had been shown 'should be kept as a family record'. Corrections and additions were added by hand to the typescript, but some may have been inserted before it was shown. For more about the typescript, the likely date(s) of composition of the text, and the editorial treatment, see the Appendix.

3 Army records state that he was born at Southsea in 1888 and attended High School in Portsmouth and the Admiralty School at Devonport. Certain details of his time at Handsworth College appear in Christopher T. Harley, 'Our Year: Being Some Account of those Careers of those twenty-six who entered Handsworth College, Birmingham, in September 1911 [the year above Rider] and departed thence in June 1914', Methodist Archive and Research Centre [hereafter MARC], John Rylands Library, Manchester. The army records list him as attending Birmingham University but Rider does not appear in the university's degree lists. However, in 1913 Handsworth College became an affiliate of the university and students could begin a BA course, so Rider, who went to the college in 1912, narrowly missed the opportunity of joining a degree course which he could probably have completed after the war. (We are indebted for this information to Philippa Bassett, archivist, Special Collections, University of Birmingham.) A hagiographic obituary in *Minutes of the Methodist Conference 1962*, p. 197, provides details of his post-1919 ministerial career. Family records are deficient: his children and grandsons are now dead, and his grand-daughters have no letters or mementoes and few recollections, partly because, while Rider lived in Jersey from 1945 to 1960, their father was an officer in the army serving and raising a family overseas. However, it is believed that before he found a vocation in the Methodist ministry Rider had trained and worked as a draughtsman. It may be noted at this point that although hereafter the terms 'Wesleyan' and 'Methodist' are used interchangeably, in the 1910s apart from the Wesleyan Methodist church there existed smaller denominations, the Primitive Methodist, United Methodist and Welsh Calvinist Methodist churches.

4 The printed hagiography reads: 'He was appointed superintendent of the Jersey circuit ... and was twice elected a member of the Jersey States. His services on behalf of youth ... were tireless ... He came to hold an honoured place in the whole community. He was a devoted servant of the Methodist Church who spent himself to the limit of his physical capacity. His preaching was always fresh, thoughtful and arresting. As a pastor he was eagerly welcomed into every home. Throughout his eventful career he retained a modest and self-effacing spirit which endeared him to all who knew him.' Rider's account might be thought to indicate a character which predicated the tribute of the final sentences.

5 *The Old Contemptible. Official Organ of the Old Contemptibles' Association*, no. 286, November 1957, pp. 1–2. The article, 'Armistice in the Field (1918)' is unsigned, but was found among Rider's papers and the initials R.J.R. had been added in

INTRODUCTION

pencil at the end. It is included in this edition as Chapter 17. We have searched the 1950s issues of this journal but found no other material likely to have been contributed by Rider. However, we note that other contributors adopted a literary style and a tone about the war similar in a number of respects to Rider's. But it is not unlikely that the contribution, even if revised in 1957, was written much earlier and formed part of the text now printed, to which it has again been conjoined.

6 The same issue of the magazine contained a resolution of the Association's 1957 conference, to the effect that the layout and contents of the magazine were to be 'so altered as to make the journal one of appeal to all Chums'. The resolution had been voted on by only 65 members, and no doubt it was the declining number of genuine 'Old Contemptibles' which had led the Association to welcome, as it appears, other 'Chums', for instance 'Pals'. It was probably this context of wider confraternity that encouraged Rider to contribute his article.

7 Even before volunteers were recruited, large numbers of men in the Reserves (i.e. ex-soldiers) or Territorials (i.e. civilians with some occasional part-time military training) had been called to the colours. War was declared on 4 August and by the end of the month Birmingham men in these categories were fighting in France. Volunteers (i.e. civilians without any military training) were recruited to form the 'New Army', after an appeal by Lord Kitchener, Secretary of State for War, issued on 8 August. War propaganda was intense and several thousand Birmingham men of all classes volunteered during August, before the Pals battalions were formed. The term 'Pals' persists: see Teletext/Connect/Service Pals.

8 Terry Carter, *Birmingham Pals: 14th, 15th and 16th (Service) Battalions of the Royal Warwickshire Regiment* [hereafter cited as Carter], Barnsley, 1997, pp. 35, 40, 52, 182. A recruiting poster similarly invited 'young fellows of better standing and education' (ibid., p. 76). The description in the text applies to the other ranks; the officers at first came from a more exalted, military-acquainted background. (The Bickersteth brother who was killed, see note 1 above, was an officer in a Leeds Pals battalion.) It is, nevertheless, noteworthy, and perhaps significant in respect of Rider's interest and approach, that when he presents dialogue between himself and other 'Pals' in the text, the Pals are not depicted as middle-class conversationalists of equal intellectual standing with the author, but as men fluent yet limited in verbal expression and mental sophistication, in other words, as fairly stereotyped 'working-class' characters. (In fact the Pals and the artillerymen of the later dialogues are not distinguished in this respect.) However, this may not have been entirely class affectation and literary convention, since by 1916 the Pals battalions may well have had their original 'educated' intake diluted by out-transfer and the intake of less well-educated elements. The accents represented in Rider's dialogues do not include an obvious 'Brummagen' accent – but Rider, who certainly grew up on the South Coast, may have lived in the Midlands only after he joined Handsworth College. (The poet Wilfred Owen similarly has his ordinary soldiers speaking in a sort of stage sub-cockney, and not in the accents of either his Merseyside upbringing or his Manchester regiment.)

9 The battalion had filled up with volunteers by mid-September, but commissions and transfers produced large gaps, so more men were taken in. Rider's army ser-

vice number, 1041, shows that he was not among the earliest volunteers (Terry Carter, personal communication), but he may have enlisted before B Company left Birmingham for training, on 5 October (Carter, pp. 42, 53).

10 We are much indebted to Terry Carter for providing us, in February 2000, with copies of these documents – and for other information additional to that in his book. We have been unable to identify Rider exactly on this photograph, as we have for comparison only a Second World War photograph of him in chaplain's uniform, although we can suggest three likely candidates.

11 By the date of the later list, probably only a few weeks after the photograph was taken, two of Rider's college pals had become lance-corporals. A 'corporal's examination' was being expected as early as 10 October 1914 (Carter, p. 58). Rider may only have won promotion when in France, but the first reference to 'the Corporal' is in an episode to be dated to early 1916 (Chapter 3), not long after the battalion's arrival in France.

12 By men being commissioned, the First Battalion lost 50 of its recruits within three months and 400 within a year (Carter, p. 65). For Rider as a specialist, see the text below; and for his apparent company transfer, see note 40 below.

13 J.E.B. Fairclough, *The First Birmingham Battalion in the Great War 1914-1919: Being a History of the 14th (Service) Battalion of the Royal Warwickshire Regiment* [hereafter Fairclough], Birmingham, 1933. While supplying much detail about the battalion, such as its honours and casualty lists, Fairclough says little about himself; his post-war career has not been traced (Carter, p. 272). An anecdote on p. 50 of his book may indicate that by mid-1916 he had risen to the rank of sergeant.

14 For these events, attacks of 23 and 30 July 1916, see Carter, pp. 104–11, 132–7, 172–86, 194–6; Fairclough, pp. 35–40, 41–52. In the first, the 14th had 194 killed and 291 wounded (Carter, p. 178)

15 Names (and army numbers) in the 1915 list mentioned have been compared with the list of deaths during the war in Carter, pp. 278–85; Fairclough, pp. 191–210. The second-in-command and the company sergeant major of B Company and the platoon sergeant of Platoon VI, as of mid-1915, were also killed in 1915–1916.

16 Carter, p. 219; Fairclough, pp. 67–76. The 1916 Somme campaign is detailed in J.E. Edmonds, *Military Operations. France and Belgium, 1916* [up to 1 July], and Wilfrid Miles, *Military Operations. France and Belgium, 1916* [from 2 July], in the series 'History of the Great War based on Official Documents', London, 1932, 1938. These works helped to create a received view of the campaign, as follows. It being mistakenly believed that previous artillery fire would have neutralised enemy wire, forward trenches and machine-gun posts, British soldiers were sent, heavily equipped and 'at a steady pace', in waves, across wide open stretches between the two front lines, and, the artillery bombardment having been inadequate, were consistently cut down by enfilading machine-gun fire (Miles, *Military Operations*, pp. 563–73). On this interpretation, the fault of the High Command was less in initiating the tactic than in persisting in it after the first failures. (The only contemporary and inter-war justification was that, perhaps surprisingly, German casualties, although fewer than those of the British, were still considerable, caused as much by shells, mines and sniping rifle fire as by face-to-face combat in up-and-at-'em bayonet assaults – hence, in this 'war of attrition', when circumstances changed, notably by the threatened battlefield arrival of large

numbers of fairly effective American troops, Germany lost and was forced to surrender.) The slaughter among front-line officers was as high as, or higher than, that among the other ranks, but, again on the received view, the survivors do not seem to have grasped the error, at least to the extent of alerting the High Command rather than merely continuing to obey orders. The false optimism of the High Command even reached down to the trench soldiery, who seem seldom or never to have protested at being called on to commit likely suicide. In Chapter 3, however, Rider's companions do express doubts about the war. Further, Rider describes in Chapter 11, perhaps somewhat over-optimistically, the advantage of one assault modification, the creeping barrage. However, the above received view about the overall folly of the enterprise has latterly been challenged, on the grounds that a broader assessment (considering, e.g., the relief of military pressure on the French at Verdun, the position on other battle fronts, political pressures in France and Britain, the lack of a possible alternative strategy) made the form of campaign inevitable and in the final analysis successful (see the relevant articles in Brian Bond, ed., *The First World War and British Military History*, Oxford, 1991).

17 Cited in G.T. Bigg, 'Notes on the beginnings of Chaplaincy Work', file history of the Army Chaplaincy, MARC, Box 36. It is also noted in O.S. Watkins, *Soldiers and Preachers: Being the Romantic Story of Methodism in the British Army, with a complete record of Wesleyan Chaplains to the Forces*, London, 1906, reprinted 1981, p. 84, where it appears to be attributed to a speaker at the 1859 Methodist Conference. The early chapters of Watkins' book attempt, however, to show that Wesley and early Methodists were not hostile to patriotism and even military service. Watkins, himself a Wesleyan chaplain, had already written two books about chaplain service in the Nile and Boer campaigns, and was to write one on his service in the early months of the 'Great War'.

18 The middle chapters of Watkins, *Soldiers and Preachers*, give an account of the Methodist campaign for recognition by the army, that is, the right of Methodist soldiers to withdraw from compulsory Anglican church parades, and the appointment of Wesleyan chaplains, a campaign which Watkins saw as gaining ground from the late 1850s.

19 For the history of British Army chaplaincy arrangements during World War I, see Alan C. Robinson, 'The role of British army chaplaincy during World War II', PhD thesis, University of Liverpool, 1999, chapter 1. The Nonconformist churches advanced their chaplaincy status during the war, especially after Lloyd George became Secretary for War and then Prime Minister. But the various denominations often spoiled their case by inter-feuding. For instance, in 1915 the Wesleyans deplored that, in units where there was no Wesleyan chaplain, officers had allocated the pastoral care of Wesleyan soldiers to Presbyterian chaplains (Minutes of the Wesleyan Methodist Army and Navy Board [hereafter WMANB], 25.6.1915). For an account by a Wesleyan chaplain of his activities in the first few months of the war, see O.S. Watkins, *With French in France and Flanders: being the experiences of a chaplain attached to a field ambulance*, London, 1915.

20 *Methodist Times*, 12.11.1914, p. 12, letter of the Rev. J. Parton Milum.

21 *Methodist Times*, 20.8.1914, editorial 'Prepare for the New Order' [sic] by the Rev. J. Scott Lidgett.

22 Belief in an after-war uplifted moral order was of course a fairly general view among clergy of all denominations, at least in the early years of the war (e.g. 'in those who are spared to return will be found the inheritors of the new world which will soon be': Horne, *Doundney*, p. 153).
23 *Methodist Times*, 3.9.1914, p. 3. The correspondent, Bateson, was, however, the Secretary of the Wesleyan Methodist Army and Navy Board which supervised the existing Wesleyan chaplains and their activities, and in respect of these liaised with the War Office.
24 *Methodist Times*, 12.11.1914, p. 12, 'Ministerial Students and Enlistment', letter from the Rev. J.T. East.
25 *Methodist Times*, 3.12.1914, p. 10.
26 It might, however, be argued that, by the time he wrote, Rider knew that the voluntary enlistment of 1914 had been followed by conscription in early 1916, when, if still a student, he would have been unlikely to have been exempted, and if already a minister might have found himself in an agonising dilemma.
27 *Methodist Times*, 31.12.1914, p. 6 'Handsworth College in War-Time'; *Methodist Times*, 29.10.1914, p. 8. Some of those who opted for the RAMC may have been considered medically unfit to join combatant units, for instance, through wearing spectacles (see P. E. H. Hair, '59206 (RAMC): Malta 1917–1918', *Medical Historian*, 10, 1998, note 10).
28 Fairclough, pp. 64–5. Fairclough does not elsewhere mention chaplains. Although the anecdote suggests that Fairclough did not personally know the four departees, it implies that they were known to Fairclough's mates and therefore that they were drawn from the same unit and had not merely met up for transfer. The four were certainly known to each other and probably friends; they were Rider, E. Foster, H. T. P. Young, and G. Rigby-Jones, all Handsworth College students. All had been in the same platoon in 1914/1915, and, excepting Rider, the others may have continued to serve in this platoon. A fifth Handsworth College member of the 1914/1915 platoon, G.E. Johnson, who by 1916 may have been elsewhere in the army, was also summoned back, but apparently a little later, since he was commissioned as a chaplain in January 1917. The later army service of these four other Handsworth students has not been traced.
29 Chapter 6, final paragraph. Elsewhere, however, the account states that 'appointment as a chaplain' was 'offered' to the Corporal, implying that Rider could have rejected it and continued in the infantry. But perhaps this would have been to defy the wishes of the authorities of his church, with unfavourable consequences. An editorial comment in the *Bickersteth Diaries* to the effect that 'throughout the war, all chaplains were volunteers' (p. 319) applies specifically to Anglican chaplains and seems to claim rather too much for 'all chaplains'.
30 By March 1915 there were estimated to be 80,000 Wesleyans in the army (WMANB, 22.3.1915).
31 Anglican chaplains also had the disadvantage of being generally of a higher social class than the typical soldier and of having often practised pastoral care, not in an urban community, but in an especially deferential rural community. It is perhaps significant that Rider does not mention encountering Anglican chaplains, either when an infantryman or when a chaplain himself. (Bickersteth, the Anglican chaplain, however, several times recorded that he encountered a 'Wesleyan padre':

e.g. *Bickersteth* JB, p. 80; moreover, Watkins, a Wesleyan chaplain serving in the early months of the war, noted that he regularly worked alongside an Anglican chaplain, to the extent that they shared services: Watkins, *With French*, passim). Rider notes that 'no Padre had been able to visit the unit for months, owing to the scarcity of chaplains' (Chapter 3). There was indeed such a scarcity. In July 1915 the number of chaplains to a division of some 20,000 men, in several different regiments and special units scattered over a wide area, was ten (seven C. of E., two R.C. and a Nonconformist); chaplains spent much time travelling but one unit had not had a chaplain visit or a service for four months (Horne, *Doundney*, pp. 145, 155). Even in June 1917 Bickersteth was to complain of only six Anglican chaplains to a division (*Bickersteth* JB, p. 181). However, there is evidence of a church parade for Rider's battalion on 19 December 1914 ('in a field just behind where our guns were banging away'), as well as of two al fresco services on Christmas Day in noisy cafés, one a communion service (Carter, pp. 119–20), and presumably it was Anglican chaplains who conducted these services. Rider may well have been unable to escape this compulsory church parade, and probably many later ones, and although a Methodist he may even have voluntarily attended the Christmas communion service. It was therefore not correct that the battalion had not seen a chaplain 'for months', and since it is unlikely that Rider was referring specifically to a Methodist chaplain he was exaggerating the position, perhaps in mis-recollection, in order to explain his own adoption of a ministerial role in organising services and acting as a 'preacher'. At a later date, when Rider was still serving as an infantryman on the Somme front, a photograph taken on 30 July shows wounded soldiers of his 14th battalion being tended to by a chaplain, of uncertain denomination, who is apparently filling in personal particulars on a Field Postcard to be sent to relatives (Carter, p. 197). (When he became a senior chaplain, Bickersteth instructed his subordinates to 'take postcards in their hands and write to the relatives of wounded men a few lines, either from dictation or in their own words': *Bickersteth* JB, p. 203). Of the 3,000 or so chaplains who 'by the end of the war had been sent to the theatre of war, 176 had given their lives' (Edmonds, *Military Operations*, p. 137) – but this was of course a relatively small proportion.

32 WMANB, 29.5.1916. Three of Rider's fellow College students (but most likely of an earlier admission year) had been commissioned as chaplains in 1914, and probably other Methodist training colleges similarly released students to be army chaplains, but the total number must have been small. Of the 27 Handsworth College students who finished training in June 1914, before war broke out, 14 subsequently became chaplains, presumably being recruited from circuit ministries (Hartley, 'Our Year', MARC).

33 Similarly, Rider wrote of chaplaincies being offered to 'qualified ministers and clergy, then serving as combatants', such as himself (Chapter 7). The significance of students who had not finished training being nevertheless regarded as 'ministers' and even as 'qualified ministers' is not clear to us. However, the Corporal described himself as having been, before enlistment, a 'preacher' (Chapter 3), that is, presumably, an authorised lay preacher, and as such he had no doubt on occasions taken services as well as preached, before and during his training. In 1906, Watkins paid tribute to the Methodist lay preachers in the army, mainly NCOs

(Watkins, *Soldiers and Preachers*, chapter VII); but Rider does not mention encountering any. Strictly, all chaplains recruited during the war, and also the full-time Wesleyan chaplains before the war, were listed as 'acting chaplains' (Edmonds, *Military Operations*, pp. 134–8).

34 The dates are from army records. While in England Rider was posted to the Home Counties Division, and conceivably he was attached to the artillery regiment which after some months was sent to France. In contrast to Rider's experience, Anglican chaplains were normally men with previous pastoral experience in a parish, and thus had the advantage of having been already in a position of administrative, social and spiritual authority. Whatever Rider did otherwise in England in later 1916, he most probably did some courting, since he married in June 1918, probably his next period in England. When a soldier looks forward to spending leave in England with his girl, at Brighton, the Padre responds: 'So would I – with my own, of course!' (Chapter 9).

35 Moreover, he claimed that in two years of chaplaincy service, he was 'almost without having had any contact whatsoever with a Padre of any kind' (Chapter 6). This is difficult to accept, although it may well have been the case that Anglican chaplains failed to contact any Methodist chaplain working within the same army section (but cf. *Bickersteth* JB, p. 248, where a Wesleyan was allowed to assist at an Anglican Communion, exceptionally; and Watkins' experience in 1914, note 31 above), and Methodist chaplains were too few to be regularly in contact with each other.

36 The pagination of the extant typescript suggests that two chapters describing his enlistment and training, if not abandoned on second thoughts as less relevant, were either lost or accidentally destroyed.

37 Carter, chapter 4.

38 Carter, p. 99. That the battalion in training, having for practice merely a dysfunctional machine-gun of German origin, was reduced to using football supporters' rattles to represent the gun in action (Carter, p. 69), was pleasing history for the senior editor, who, in 1944, for much the same reason, was similarly entrusted with a rattle during Home Guard exercises.

39 Rider is named in the 'Daily Orders' of 14 January 1915, as 'one of those qualified as Class 1 Semaphore Signalling and therefore to attend a daily signalling class' (Terry Carter pers. comm.). It is not known if Rider had any special technical qualification which led to his selection as a signalman, although the tasks required, on the technical side, little more than an elementary knowledge of electrical functions, a knowledge which could be imparted quickly to an ignoramus. However, as Rider's account proves, the signalman worked individually, often in highly dangerous circumstances, and carried a measure of responsibility towards his own and larger units, therefore the selection may have been by character (and perhaps originally by intelligence in coping with semaphore). In 1914–1916, effective battlefield communication was mainly by telephone, or when that failed by runner or despatch rider. Many other methods existed, notably visual communication by semaphore in daytime, by Morse lamp at night, also by 'flags, rockets, flares, coloured smoke', even by pigeons (as carried later by tanks); but these other methods were generally in decline. Although the navy used wireless from the start of the war, the army front line was slower to adopt it and use it effectively – Rider

does not mention it. The signalman's main task was therefore, first to lay out the telephone wires between the command posts and the front line or any advance posts (cf. 'laying out a wire between the headquarters and the assaulting force'; Chapter 6; 'out laying wires', Chapter 1), including wires laid loosely along trenches, and then to mend the wires when enemy shells broke them, as happened frequently (cf. 'a shell had ... broken the wires', Chapter 1). By 1916 it had become normal to 'bury' the wires leading back from the front line, increasingly more deeply (which was perhaps why 'the Corporal' was digging a trench, Chapter 4). Hence the signalman often worked under fire. For two signallers, members of a raiding party (of the 15th battalion), see Carter, p. 144. For a detailed discussion of the Signal Service, see Edmonds, *Military Operations*, pp. 67–73, 286; and for elaborate instructions issued by the General Staff in February 1916, *Military Operations. France and Belgium, 1916* [up to 1 July], *Appendices* volume, pp. 95–6. The signalman's routine tasks, although contributing to battlefield combat, did not involve direct wounding or killing, and it is likely that signalmen often did not carry weapons – and were then rather like chaplains (for the Padre pretending to carry a gun, see Chapter 12). However, Rider describes an episode when two signalmen were among five soldiers trapped in a front-line trench during a German attack, and how they prepared to beat off any assault on their 'strong point', 'shoulder to shoulder at the parapet', the signallers without guns but with 'six Mills bombs each' (Chapter 4). No doubt in other emergencies signallers would use rifles. It is therefore highly unlikely that Rider's selection as a signaller, inasmuch as he had any role in the selection (which is unlikely), involved any thought on his part that the duties were less combatant than those of most soldiers.

40 According to Fairclough, just before the battalion left for France signallers were transferred from other companies to D Company (Fairclough, p. 19); and in France signallers were transferred to a Headquarters Company within the battalion (Carter, p. 106). Rider records that at one point 'the Corporal went to Company Headquarters' (Chapter 3). It therefore seems that the subsequent history of B Company does not apply to Rider (see note 43 below). The battalion also hived off a separate machine-gun section (Carter, p. 69), this being mentioned in Chapter 4.

41 Fairclough, who participated in these marches, is eloquent about their ardours: Fairclough, pp. 31–2. The number who fell out is from Carter, p. 100. However, Rider says that he sought the dentist only after the company had halted and the men been dismissed.

42 The mud is celebrated at length in Fairclough, pp. 36, 39–40.

43 Fairclough, pp. 51–2 ('our stay in the Arras front had been interesting' [!]); Carter, pp. 153–4. Rider's account of the mine incident and the aftermath is puzzling. The 14th and 15th Warwickshires were neighbours in the front line near Arras on 4 June, preparing to be relieved the next day, when, after heavy shelling of the 15th all day, at 9.30 p.m. three German mines were exploded, two harmlessly but one under a section of the position of the 15th, and this was instantly followed by a German raid. All told, over sixty men of the 15th were killed, a number being entombed. D Company of the 14th was the immediate neighbour of the 15th. According to Fairclough, the 14th suffered casualties that were 'comparatively light, mainly in D Company' (probably not as a result of the mine but in tackling the raiding party). Both battalions were relieved the next day. But work parties

were sent back to restore the damaged positions. These included parties from the 14th, who found 'dugouts had been smashed in ... [but] bodies of men of the 15th Royal Warwickshires were recovered for burial [who] in many cases had enlisted together for the City Battalions' (Fairclough, p. 51). Rider's reference reads as if his battalion, the 14th, was the one principally attacked, and as if his company (which was probably by then D Company, rather than the earlier B Company) was the one whose men were entombed, both claims being incorrect. It is plausible, however, that a 14th battalion work party from D Company, which had been close to the explosion, under Rider as corporal, returned 'early next morning' to dig for the entombed men of the 15th, by specific permission, and even that some men volunteered for this, given that the 15th was also a Pals battalion from Birmingham. Carter states that 'eight still lie to this day, in a collapsed dugout forty feet underneath the ground' (Carter, p. 154).

44 Fairclough, pp. 49, 51. The battalion after Rider left it returned twice to Roclincourt, so Fairclough knew it well. The drawings (included in this edition) appear to be originals, one being dated '1916'. Rider marked them for insertion as illustrations in his account. They perhaps testify to an earlier career as a draughtsman. For a photograph of a cellar dugout entrance in Roclincourt in April 1916, see Carter, p. 140.

45 Fairclough, p. 50. Rider wrote that British trenches ran through an unnamed village and 'a small cemetery shadowed by the ruins of a shattered church' (Chapter 1) – this was probably also Roclincourt. Chaplain Bickersteth, at a later date (January 1917), was impressed by a similar sight. 'In the utterly strafed village, close by here, is a remarkable sight. In the churchyard, alone, in solitary grandeur, stands a lofty Crucifix ... Only low pieces of the wall of the church remain standing. What stumps of trees remain are charred and bereft of every branch' (*Bickersteth* JB, p. 154).

46 Fairclough, pp. 41–3. This was at Vaux-sur-Somme. For photographs of Vaux, probably taken after the war but the houses and streets still looking very backwoods, see Fairclough, opposite p. 52; and for a photograph of French troops marching along an unmade road between houses in Vaux, see Carter, p. 125.

47 Earlier Rider had participated in 'a kind of service in the barn at our billet' (Chapter 3), perhaps a prayer meeting organised by a number of men who were Methodists, but Rider does not claim to have taken a lead in this activity.

48 Fairclough, narrating the early 1916 period of the battalion's history, has an anecdote about a clumsy signaller in relation to a project to 'lay a cable parallel to the front line in order to tap German signals by induction', and to actual wiring when two out of a party of three signallers from B Company were seriously wounded and had to be rescued. But a later reference to 'Bob the signaller' cannot be to Rider as it relates to December 1916 (Fairclough, pp. 49, 83).

49 As it happened, the 14th Warwickshires participated in the successful attack, and it is possible that Rider managed a contact with his former infantry battalion, although probably few of his 'pals' had survived.

50 See Chapter 15, note 1.

51 An attempt in 1916 to order chaplains to go no nearer the front than the advanced dressing-stations led to protest and was withdrawn (Edmonds, *Military Operations*, p. 138).

INTRODUCTION

52 The citation in the *Supplement to the London Gazette* of 22.6.1918 read as follows: 'The Rev. Robert John Rider, Army Chaplains Department. For conspicuous gallantry and devotion to duty. Hearing that some wounded men were lying out in the open, he obtained and led stretcher parties for four of these wounded men, and being unable to procure additional help, carried in the fifth man himself along an exposed road, during which period he was on several occasions compelled to take cover. His gallantry and coolness cannot be too highly praised.' The presentation tends to be formulaic since there were many awards for similar actions, but the reference to 'coolness' is perhaps unusual. Rider commended himself for facing 'stern ordeals calmly' (Chapter 7). The statement that the incident occurred at 'Poel Capelle' appears in the Methodist obituary (note 3 above). Poelkappelle, north of Ypres, was gained by the British in the Passchendaele campaign of October 1917 and lost again when the line was adjusted because of the German offensive further south, on 13–14 April 1918 (J.E. Edmonds, *Military Operations. France and Belgium 1918 (March)*, London, 1937, p. 245). Assuming that the award was made not longer than two months after the action, Rider's exploit took place in early April 1918, immediately before the switch of his unit to the Lys front. He was married (which also is not noted in his account) a few days before the award was gazetted, so was on leave in England when it was announced. His present-day descendants were unaware of the award. Rider's reticence about his award may have been because he shared an opinion with Chaplain Bickersteth, who also was awarded the MC but who wrote – 'I am sorry about it. I hold strong views about chaplains' decorations. They never have "to go over the top"; they have a comparatively easy job from the military point of view' (*Bickersteth* JB, p. 228).

53 In fairness, non-combatant status seems to have been ill-defined – perhaps inevitably in modern war. When in 1916 a Non-Combatant Corps of conscientious objectors was formed, their assigned duties included loading and unloading ships and vehicles, and also digging, provided it was not in the front line (Edmonds, *Military Operations*, pp. 67–8). Chaplain Watkins, serving in the early months of the war, also undertook billeting duties, together with an Anglican colleague (Watkins, *With French*, p. 92).

54 The account does not specify this, but the billeting duties noted in Chapters 16 and 17 may indicate that, even if he was still attached to the artillery, he was being deployed in the now rapid advance of the Division's infantry. If so, a possible explanation is as follows. Nonconformist chaplains being rarer than Anglican chaplains, they could accept some pastoral responsibility for a wider unit than the regiment to which they were formally attached, that is, to the Division. In the circumstances of a headlong advance, the Division may have deployed Rider for billeting duties with the forward infantry, these being ahead of his own artillery unit.

55 After malaria and shell shock, 'the worst remaining [medical] scourge was venereal disease, which affected something like one man in five. The military authorities had no previous experience in dealing with a mass army and tried to pretend for some time that their men were only a little lower than the angels. French cooperation in organising brothels, with some rudimentary medical control, was not enlisted until 1916; protective sheaths were not issued until 1917' (A.J.P. Taylor, *English History 1914–1945*, 1965, p. 121). Possibly the compromise in morals to

which the Padre confessed (Chapter 7) related to the provision and distribution of condoms – although during his chaplaincy Rider became a married man and may therefore have been less personally involved in invoking pre-marital celibacy. Coincidentally, Rider used the same phrase as Taylor, 'a little lower than the angels', but used it, as the final statement of his account, with a very different undertone.

56 A photograph of soldiers recovering a paybook from a corpse, Carter, p. 185.
57 See note 31 above for a reference to a photograph of a chaplain doing just this.
58 Cf. 'My work is the same most days – with the wounded in the Aid-posts and Dressing Stations, burying the dead, visiting the living, writing to the bereaved, eating, sleeping, reading a little, praying a little. Only very seldom do I get the chance of holding services' (*Bickersteth* JB, p. 172). Admittedly, this was written during a period of active battle. In the early months of the war, the Methodist chaplain Watkins, with an Anglican colleague, was attached to a field ambulance unit, and spent much time in dressing stations and in evacuating the wounded, but 'we frequently grieve that there is so little [else] we can do' (Watkins, *With French*, p. 108).
59 Rider prepared a few pages of illustrations to accompany his text, most being picture postcards of destroyed buildings, with moralising captions added in hand. (The postcards having been torn out of an album, the text on the reverse side of the pictures supplying the identification of the places is obscured and not legible.) One picture has the caption '"Conventional Christianity": A German church parade'. This was clearly a reflection of Rider's lack of enthusiasm for the compulsory church parades of any army. The Anglican chaplain Bickersteth, although taking many church parades himself and at first keen on multiplying them, eventually wrote that he was 'becoming less and less enamoured of the compulsory Church Parades' (*Bickersteth* JB, p. 116).
60 Although the brothers Bickersteth recognised 'the courage, self-sacrifice and endurance of countless numbers of these men' (*Bickersteth* JB, p. 101), it is notable that, compared to Rider, they have much less to say about 'comradeship'. Neither had served in the ranks in France.
61 Whereas chaplain Bickersteth, whose theology laid great weight on church worship in the form of response to priestly-mediated sacramental mysteries, spoke sourly of mere chumminess: 'Any padre can go about and be pleasant among officers and men' – although he did allow himself to 'chat up and down the lines daily with the men and in huts and billets' (*Bickersteth* JB, p. 84).
62 Chaplain Bickersteth wrote a number of friendly and even admiring references to Roman Catholic individuals and religious practices (e.g. *Bickersteth* JB, pp. 71–2, 253), but this came more easily to him as he was a High (sacramentalist) Anglican.
63 Chaplain Bickersteth, although himself 'public school', complained that 'the average old public school officer disregards entirely, with one or two exceptions, his responsibility to his men from a spiritual point of view. He makes it his business to see that the men under his charge have enough to eat, and are warm and dry, as far as possible, but he doesn't seem to imagine that they also have souls' (*Bickersteth* JB, p. 83). An editorial summary in the *Bickersteth Diaries* notes that when a padre suggests services 'the officers say "Yes, padre, it would do the men good", but do not turn up themselves' (p. 76).

64 The reference to 'sob stuff' may, however, have been a dig at the emotional religiosity of some Nonconformist practice.
65 Whereas by September 1916, appalled by the Somme slaughter which had included the death of their younger brother, the brothers Bickersteth, both chaplain Julian and his cavalry officer brother Burgon, were taking a view of the war whose balance was markedly negative. Julian, distressed by the 'blood, blood, blood' of the dressing stations he had worked in, wrote as follows. 'This War may bring out some of the good qualities in man, but the evil it does is incalculably greater. The whole thing is utterly devilish ... our whole moral outlook is being systematically lowered.' Burgon wrote: 'after the war I shall write a book, and in it I shall put everything that is filthy and disgusting and revolting and degrading and terrifying about modern warfare – and hope thereby to do my bit towards preventing another'. And a little later he questioned whether the war should continue: 'is the thing we are fighting worse than the methods we are forced to use in trying to fight it?' (*Bickersteth* JB, p. 137; *Bickersteth* BB, pp. 147-9). Even Watkins, the Methodist chaplain who recorded service only in the first months of the war (and originally recorded it for printing in the *Methodist Recorder*), while he began by narrating, unlike Rider, much detail of patriotic military movements, eventually interspersed his account with darker reflections, referring to the 'devilish wickedness of war', redeemed only by the 'golden thread of the magnificent bravery of our men' (Watkins, *With French*, p. 136).
66 It is a curious coincidence that one of the War Poets' most desperate, effective and acclaimed poems concerns a 'Jim' who does return from the battlefield but —' 'E reckoned 'e'd five chances, an' 'e 'ad; / 'E's wounded, killed, and pris'ner, all the lot, / The bloody lot all rolled in one. Jim's mad.' (Wilfred Owen, 'The Chance').
67 He does preach to German prisoners of war but we are not told what he said (Chapter 13).
68 The term 'Great War' probably had, for Rider, Bunyanesque and Puritan undertones of the Great War against Evil/Sin/the Devil.
69 The effect of the battlefield on religious belief in the case of the ordinary soldiers was much discussed by churchmen and not least chaplains. Yet an extremely level-headed set of comments was produced, not by chaplain Bickersteth, but by a layman, his brother Burgon. 'Personal philanthropy, if it can be called that' had increased, but not general religious belief. 'The average British soldier is very fatalistic ... He hates to talk about his soul and resents the high patriotic tone ... He grouses interminably ... He uses filthy and abominable language, treats church parade as a parade, and does not stay to Communion as much through moral cowardice as anything else. The padre is appreciated by the men in so far as he busies himself with their recreational and physical comfort, and respected if he visits the front line and shares their danger. If he does both, he is loved. His uniform is probably more of a disadvantage than an advantage ...' (*Bickersteth* BB, pp. 168-9).
70 It finds commonplace expression in the clause of the Lord's Prayer, 'Lead us not into temptation', which liturgiologists have recently proposed to revise to 'Spare us a time of testing'.
71 It may be further noted that although the soldiers are quoted as using 'bloody' and 'damn'/'damned' (written as 'b...' and 'd...', and the former in Chapter 12 as

simply '...'), they are never cited as extending their improper language to sexual and excretory terms, not even to 'bugger', which is utterly implausible.

72 The longest anecdotes concerning 'Badger' (Chapter 8) and 'Fiz' (Chapter 15) deal with individuals presented as not only generally unattractive but also somewhat simple-minded, who are then improved in character by events. But it can be argued, in fairness, that the selection and presentation related as much to Rider's pastoral vocation and professional mission, that is, to his Christian and evangelical beliefs, as to his own character.

73 A cult of '*mores* characterized as anti-imperialist, anti-heroic, hostile towards traditional authority, and profoundly sceptical of the efficacy of force in general and war in particular to solve political problems ... though ostensibly anti-war, was more emphatically anti-authority, specifically anti upper-class authority. It was, in a word, anti-officer' (Bond, *The First World War*, pp. 8, 9; and cf. pp. 281–6).

74 The bishop pontificates: 'When the boys come back / They will not be the same; for they'll have fought / In a just cause; they lead the last attack / On Anti-Christ; their comrades' blood has bought / New right to breed an honourable race, / They have challenged Death and dared him face to face.' ('They'). These are very close to Rider's views, and were no doubt assaulted vitriolically by Sassoon precisely because they were not the exclusive banter of a bishop but were widespread in the religious community of the nation.

75 To cite Wilfred Owen, 'those who die as cattle' – 'The Poetry is in the pity'. But 'Graves, Sassoon and their ilk were nearly all officers from an educated class with an awareness of literature. To regard them as typical of the majority of men who served in the British Army between 1914 and 1918 is probably quite misleading' (Simkins in Bond, *The First World War*, p. 312). It is certainly a moot point whether Sassoon and Owen, despite being dissident, 'neurasthenic' members of the officers' mess, quite overcame their social and educational background when writing of the ordinary soldiery, since their poetry was intended to appeal to the poetry-reading intelligentsia, with the purpose of persuading this elite to abandon the current way it ran the world and produced wars. Although Rider too was not exactly typical, his religious attachment, perhaps especially within the Nonconformist tradition, and his non-literary background, made him arguably more understanding.

76 'The gulf between them [those who fought in the 1914–1918 war] and the people of the 1990s is already virtually unbridgeable, and widens every day' (Terraine, in the Introduction to *The Bickersteth Diaries*, p. ix).

77 At one point he excuses 'Headquarters' for persisting in an unsuccessful and devastating attack (Chapter 4), but probably in this particular instance the excuse is just.

78 For a glowing appraisal from the literary angle, true to the 1960s, see D.J. Enright, 'The Literature of the First World War', in Boris Ford, ed., *The Modern Age* (The Pelican Guide to English Literature 7), Harmondsworth, 1961. This 'War Rage' was undoubtedly a major influence on certain quarters of British public opinion in the inter-war decades but whether this literature trickled down to the level of Nonconformist ministers such as Rider is unclear, and its anti-religious content may have immunised them from it.

79 They appear to date to before the Somme battles and at least in part should prob-

ably be instead dated to after the first. The Bickersteth brothers utter explicitly negative comments on the war in September 1916, just as Rider was leaving the infantry.
80 The objection to bayoneting an enemy is repeated in Chapter 6. Cf. 'But for the most part, they are not wildly enthusiastic about shoving a bayonet into the stomach of a fair-haired German boy about their same age and imbued with much the same ideas on war as themselves' (*Bickersteth* BB, p. 149).
81 See Martin Caedel, *Pacificism in Britain 1914–45*, London, 1980.
82 Among a few loose manuscript pages accompanying the typescript is one giving a suggested title page, 'The Fight and the Fighters. By a Padre'.

Chapter 1

Trenches and Mines

Being in the trenches is not the same proposition in all parts of the line. There are some sections of the line where everything is wet, muddy and uncomfortable and where perforce the defence works have to be of sandbags above the ground rather than of trenches dug into it. Other sectors gain the reputation of being 'cushy parts' by reason of their having deep trenches in clean, dry earth. In the latter case, conditions of living are considerably better in almost every particular, the chalky sub-soil making it possible for men to enjoy the luxury of dugout life. In war, however, one can be sure that every good thing has some snag about it. Favourable conditions will be exploited to secure some military advantage over the enemy. In this case, the dryness and rigidity of the ground make possible a new use of Mother Earth.

Opposing trenches in this part of the line approached to within 45 yards of each other, near enough to permit conversation between the rival outposts. It made possible the use of short-range weapons, trench mortars and hand-grenades. There was always the possibility of 'surprise arrivals' of many kinds from the enemy lines.

A company of men in khaki arrived in the area and their unusually small physique caused some speculation about their usefulness for frontline work. It was learned that they had been recruited from the ranks of the coal-miners at home and this qualified them for a special kind of service in sections such as this. These men were set to work some distance back along the communication trench, and from here they began tunnelling underground. The passage they built headed towards the enemy lines, running beneath 'no-man's-land' to a point underneath the enemy dugouts. Even with all precautions taken, it was impossible to carry through such work undetected, sound being the chief revealer of these evil designs. Once detected, retaliation along similar lines was inevitable, and it therefore became a race between rival parties of miners to forestall each other in reaching the best position for effective action.[1]

Tommy became aware, by an uncanny instinct, that his own position was being undermined, and a few days later it was confirmed by the incessant, unmistakable 'Tap-Tap, Tap-Tap, Thud-Thud' from somewhere below. Trying to sleep with such an accompaniment, and with the knowledge that only a few yards of earth separated one from the picks and shovels of enemy tunnellers, was a new test of courage. To know that one was sandwiched between possible prowling patrols on the surface paying their respects with bombs and grabbing tactics, and the attentions of enemy sappers underground, meant that Tommy had to practise a new stoicism in dealing with the 'new risks'. Without this spirit of apparent unconcern, his existence would have been as unpleasant as it was insecure.

'Jock', a dour Scotsman, usually the quiet member of the platoon, met the situation by supplying a bit of sound philosophy. 'There they are again, Bill!', said he to his pal, 'Listen!' The unmistakable 'Tap-Tap, Tap-Tap, Thud-Thud' could be plainly heard.

'D'ye know Bill, I've got to like that noise', said Jock.

'Liar!', came in response.

'Aye, I have, Bill! Look here, it's like this. While those blighters are digging they ain't loadin' up with dynamite, and that's the only thing that really concerns us or can do us any harm. It shows they ain't finished yet. It's when they stops and it's all quiet that you don't know what the teffles are up to.'[2]

---

1 Once the initial German campaign – through Belgium and towards Paris and then in 'the race to the sea' – had halted, two lines of facing trenches were drawn across NW France and SW Belgium. Breakthrough being almost impossible, as was learned bloodily, one form of assault common to both sides was by tunnelling under the enemy positions and exploding 'mines'. (A recent popular novel dealing with the 1914–1918 war provides references to such explosions and the consequent entombment of British soldiers: Sebastian Faulks, *Birdsong*, 1993.) The most spectacular and probably the most devastating use of mines was when the British exploded 500 tons of ammonal to destroy German positions on the Messines ridge covering the Arras front, on 7 June 1917. 'Nineteen mines were simultaneously exploded, blowing the top of the hill into the air and in places entirely altering its contours' (C.R.M.F. Cruttwell, *A History of the Great War 1914–1918* [hereafter Cruttwell], Oxford, 1934, pp. 436–8 – although many later and more detailed studies of the Western Front have appeared, Cruttwell has the advantage of having been himself a combatant in France. Rider is describing mining on the Arras front in Spring 1916.

2 Rider makes some attempt at Jock's Scottish dialect. However, 'Aye' appears in later dialogue when the speaker is not obviously Scottish and in one instance (Chapter 9) is even Rider himself. This seems implausible in actuality and more a literary convention. The other term, 'teffles', for 'devils', would seem to represent Jock as a Gaelic-speaking Highlander, rightly or wrongly.

'Tap-Tap, Tap-Tap, Thud-Thud' came persistently but now encouragingly. Bill began to whistle cheerfully, grateful to Jock for his bit of sound logic; he felt ever afterwards that he could afford to give Fritz a musical accompaniment to his labours.[3]

Thus passed the days and nights in that sector, and it was only when the sounds ceased that the men were inclined to be meditative. Periodically quite extended silences came, and then things took on an air of foreboding expectancy. Not even the suggestion that Fritz 'had gone on strike for a rise', or that 'the British sappers had met them underground and that they were having a drink together', entirely relieved the men of anxiety. It was so certain that all the work below ground was purposeful, and that it was of evil design, that its possibilities could not be disguised or belittled.

For several days the sounds seemed to the men in the front line to be growing fainter and fainter, ending in a period of four days' complete quiet. Again there was a call upon Jock's philosophical mind. Latterly, keen listening had developed in him a particularly sensitive pair of ears. On the fourth day he entered the dugout with a broad smile on his face, for he was the bearer of good tidings. He had been sent back along the communication trench with a message for an officer in reserve and had picked up the lost sound again as he went. He noticed also that it got louder and more distinct the farther back he went. From this he inferred that the human moles, still busy, had passed right under the front line trenches and were making for a destination elsewhere. His news acted as a tonic to subconsciously apprehensive men, and they went about their work again with considerably less concern.

In a few days, however, there came an ominous silence even back in the reserve line trenches and the men sadly missed the 'Tap-Tap, Tap-Tap, Thud-Thud'. The almost inexhaustible wit of the party showed signs of giving out as the days passed. The only hope men entertained was that the prolonged stillness meant that the scheme had been abandoned, a hope they scarcely dared to consider. Days followed and the routine life of the trenches went on, but never quite carefree.[4]

One part of the British trenches in this sector ran through a village, and right across a small cemetery shadowed by the ruins of a shattered

---

3 'Fritz' is a German soldier, alternatively a 'Boche', just as a 'Tommy' is a British soldier. But 'Fritz' or 'Old Fritz', as later used, is the German soldiery, or the German war machine in general.
4 On 15 April 1916, 'the battalion was informed that they were sitting practically on top of a German mine ... "which made things a bit strained"' (Carter, p. 135, citing a diary).

church.[5] Close by, in what had been the priory, now in ruins, there was a deep cellar in which scrounging signallers had found some treasure trove which they reported to their Signals Officer. It was a group of dry electric cells in good condition, all active, which had at one time done duty as the supply for the bell circuits of the priory. The excited Signals Officer conceived the brilliant idea of confiscating them for military purposes. His suggestion was that they could be used to speed up the alarm system between the listening posts and the troops in reserve, lessening the possibility of a surprise attack. With the aid of a few willing signallers, grateful for the opportunity of doing something other than routine work, the idea was soon translated into a practical proposition.

One end of the circuit was to be in the dugout of the officer commanding the troops in the line; the other end to be within easy reach of the listening sentry. Inconspicuously on the wall of his dugout, just over the officer's head, an electric bell was placed; and a bell push was secured at the elbow of the sentry. The whole system seemed to be in sympathy with the dignified work it was to be called upon to do and the little bell responded willingly to the push. When all the tests the inventor deemed necessary had been successfully passed, the eager circuit was commissioned for service. In these conditions of unusual security a company and its officers prepared to settle down for the night. The Company Commander, quite satisfied with the resourcefulness of his Signals Officer and the reliability of the men at the 'post', relaxed his muscles and put his mind at ease. He gave instructions that he was only to be disturbed if any alarm was raised.

The alternating sounds of gurgling inhalations and hissing exhalations announced the fact that he, like some of his fellow officers, had dozed off, having snatched sleep easily through implicit trust. These sounds were acting as a dangerous lullaby to the duty officer, who was himself almost on the point of taking an expedition into slumberland but was spared such a crime by the vigorous and continuous oscillations of the bell striker. He jumped instantly into action and roused everyone within reach. Up the steps of the dugout the officers scrambled, mingling with men from an adjacent dugout who were dangerously hurrying along with fixed bayonets, eager to be in the fray. The Company Commander pushed his way past the men in front of him and took his place with the Sergeant-Major at the head of the platoon that was making its way to support the sentries in the listening post. The officer and sergeant, with loaded

---

5 Apparently the village was Roclincourt, a few miles north of Arras.

revolvers in their hands, hurried forward, looking for crouching Fritzes at every revetment in the trench. They feared they might be 'nabbed' by the body-snatching German attackers, as the sentries obviously had already been, judging by their silence.

> 'Advance friend and be recognised!' To this invitation the officer responded promptly, less than comfortable because the challenger was pointing his bayonet well out towards his chest.
> 'What the ... has happened?', said the officer when he had established his identity.
> 'Nothing, Sir!'
> 'Then why the devil did you give the alarm?'
> 'I didn't, Sir!'
> 'Someone did!'
> 'No, Sir!'

This unsatisfactory dialogue led to the inspection of the 'electrical communications'. A slight fall of earth had jammed the contacts of the bell push. The bell was still ringing in the vacated dugout, if by then showing signs of exhaustion. Although there had been the opportunity of proving the prowess of the men in the hour of emergency, the little bell, whose only fault was its too ready response to a call, was referred to as something other than a bell. The Company Commander, now back in his dugout, expressed a desire to see the Signals Officer, with whom he had a few words.

Things settled down and there was an attempt to recapture the fugitive sleep but another alarm stirred the occupants of the dugout into action again. The C.O.[6] delegated his second-in-command to investigate this time, before he stirred. There was a similar absence of excitement in the trenches and a signaller went out to make enquiries. This time a shell had dropped into the communication trench and broken the wires, which had then fallen across one another and short-circuited the system, making another call upon the services of the willing oscillator. Considerable enjoyment was got from that night's happenings when the news of the 'attack' was passed on from one man to another, with ever increasing accretions. It had relieved the monotony of things and made the opportunity for a special visit of the Signals Officer to his C.O. who, with a fitting verbal preamble, courteously but emphatically advised him to secure a better night's rest for them in future.

6 Commanding Officer.

The next night, after a quiet period on daytime alert, the men were expecting a usual night's sleep, but at midnight the 'silence', which had previously troubled the men, but had been forgotten during the happier day, yielded up its secret with a tremendous explosion. The two dugouts where the men in reserve were sleeping were completely wrecked; floors and roofs met and entombed the occupants. Nearly sixty men had been instantaneously killed, mercifully. Two signallers had been out mending wires and had escaped their comrades' fate, though they were lying half-stunned at the bottom of the trench. A shower of Verey lights lit up the scene immediately after the explosion, and this guided a raiding party of Germans, who swarmed into the crater in search of prisoners.[7] Some of the raiders jumped over the two crouching signallers at the bottom of the trench, mistaking them for sandbags or perhaps not seeing them at all. After a search of the crater and its immediate neighbourhood, the Germans retired to their line with but small quarry, as their previous work had been too well done.

Early next morning, half a company from reserve came up to relieve the few survivors of the disaster, and the remnants of the company marched back two miles behind the line for 'rest'. Some of the survivors were unhappy at having to leave their comrades entombed and were loath to accept, as a fact, that there could be no possible hope of escape for their mates. They urged the sergeant to ask the C.O. to let them return to the scene as a digging party, at least to make an effort to effect a rescue. Their keenness influenced the officer to give his permission and in half an hour a party of ten men set out with picks and shovels. Feverishly they worked for an hour in their attempt to open up the mouths of the dugouts, but meeting with no success and seeing no likelihood of it, they abandoned their self-appointed task with reluctance. Before they left, the Corporal called them to attention, and baring their heads they listened to the few and simple words of an improvised committal, which was nevertheless no less dignified than that of any more official burial in the tombs of a cathedral.[8]

Having done their best, the men knew it was useless to occupy their thoughts with the wretched business any longer, and they set out with that strange cheerfulness that accompanies acknowledged defeat. Arriv-

---

7 'At night no-man's-land, a hive of wiring activity, was lit up intermittently with flares ... [At first] the Germans surpassed the Allies both in the quantity and quality available, of lights, "star-shells" and searchlights' (Cruttwell, p. 107). The Verey light was a rocket flare.

8 For comment on this episode which the narrative in part misrepresents, see the Introduction, note 43.

ing, after nearly an hour's march, at their billets they found a hot meal awaiting them and in the enjoyment of it, the first for many hours, they began to 'bury their sorrows'. Five hours of sound sleep gave them the ministry of heroic forgetfulness and prepared them for their normal routine life again.

Chapter 2

A Minor Wound

Bob had been in the Army over twelve months and had learned through necessity to do without scores of the little luxuries and friendly considerations which his good home had previously secured for him.[1] He was by then a true, keen, and hardened soldier, and was inclined to regard a number of minor physical ailments as belonging to an elementary stage of soldiering, so that he was unwilling to own up to them when they came his way. Nothing less than wounds, received either in rough handling or by accident, and made prominent by either splints or bandages, seemed to him to be appropriate for the well-developed physique which he claimed to possess. One day, however, a less glorious disability put him out of action. He would have preferred to have concealed its presence, but there were such obvious physical accompaniments of the malady that they gave it an undue advertisement. To have a puffed-up face, occasioned by the childish complaint of toothache, was rather humiliating. But there, on the left-hand side of his jaw and fixed firmly in its socket, was a decaying back tooth, which at the time seemed to demand far more room in which to operate than did its corresponding denture on the other side.

Bob's battalion had been days on the march in France and there was no opportunity for calling at an Army Dentist's quarters for treatment. Reporting to his Regimental Medical Officer early one morning, he underwent an inspection as he sat on a box outside a temporary bivouac that had been erected at the roadside as accommodation for the previous

---

1 This chapter, although fairly inconsequential in terms of the overall serious theme of the account, is significantly autobiographical, in that the only soldier invoked is the narrator, who for once supplies his name, 'Bob'. The tone of somewhat forced humour suggests that it may have originally been intended for, or formed part of, a different text. In Rider's typescript it is marked 'An extra story not included in the MS'. The incident described must have occurred in late 1915 or early 1916. Rider had enlisted from college, but presumably did not wish to disclose this, so refers instead to the comforts of a 'good home'.

night.[2] Bob was informed that the Doctor was not equipped for dentistry, but that he did carry one pair of forceps which had done duty mostly as pliers. For ordinary local anaesthetic purposes he also carried a freezing mixture. Bob agreed to trust his fate to this scanty outfit. His gum was frozen and an unsuccessful attempt was made to extract the offending member. Thrice the gum was frozen and thrice the tooth attacked, but the tooth defied dislodgement. A psychological cure had, however, been effected, and Bob returned to duty. A few hours exhausted the usefulness of the cure, and pain as bad as ever returned to disturb the peace of the would-be hardened soldier.

For twenty-four hours extreme misery was endured. This was somewhat relieved when Bob noticed, at the last stage of the day's march, that the battalion passed a chemist's shop on whose signboard was the announcement of the auxiliary qualification of *'Dentiste'*. As only a mile separated this surgery from the halting place for the night, almost as soon as the Company was dismissed, Bob wended his way back along the road. Entering the shop, he saw the 'qualified person' doing slow-movement exercises of some kind or other behind the counter. Attracting his attention, Bob explained his mission. Invited to open his mouth for inspection, he exposed to view as much of the 'scene of future operations' as the tight skin of the cheek would allow. It was surveyed from the other side of the counter by a pair of spectacled eyes, and a knowing shake of the head seemed to signify that the seat of the trouble had at least been located. The rays of light that came into the shop were diffused by passing through a huge glass vessel of light-blue coloured water, the usual prominent symbol of the pharmacy. This light fell on the face of the dentist as he peered into the visitor's mouth, and gave him a kind of ghostly Mephistophelian hue, which in itself was enough to drive toothache away for ever. With the twice-mentioned observation that it was *'très mauvais'*, the dentist ushered the patient into his surgery, which was the living room and kitchen combined, and bade him occupy a straight-backed wooden chair placed in the centre of the room in front of the grate.

By this time the dentist's wife had become interested. She was invited to pass her judgement on the case. In the hope of getting a close-up view of the situation, she manoeuvred her eighteen stones of human flesh through a far doorway and stood over the poor fellow who was seated,

---

2 A 'bivouac' is a temporary encampment, for instance, of tents and, as here, for overnight shelter. The term was much used in World War I and later in the text appears in a shortened form as 'bivvy'.

awaiting the next move. The opportunity was grudgingly given her and she immediately confirmed the opinion of both her husband and his client. She then took a chair and mounted it, in order to reach a wooden box that had lain concealed for many a day on a top shelf in a dark corner of the room. As she took it down, she dislodged from it an eighth of an inch of accumulated dust by means of two or three substantial puffs from well-inflated cheeks and lungs. Bob's eyes surveyed the box with anxiety, and when the lid was taken off he beheld an instrument the likes of which he had never before set eyes upon, either in actuality or in illustration.

Its 'business end' was like the jaws of a claw hammer in semi-miniature. Three-quarters of an inch from the points was a right-angled turn, forming a straight shaft about five inches in length, and at the other end of this was a substantial, corkscrew handle. With this tool, it was possible to give all the varying leverages and torsion movements necessary for different operations associated with dentistry. As can be imagined, the instrument was of the greatest value when the tooth adjacent to the one to be extracted was already out and a good enfilade movement was possible. But this condition of things was not offered by the present patient's jaw, and in consequence the operation was to be a more delicate one. The claws of the weapon were pressed in to encircle Bob's tooth as near to the root as possible, the fleshy gums presenting no obstacle. A little manipulation and a few trial movements assured the doctor that all was ready for the wrench. But the grip failed. A second attempt and a second failure followed. The lady assistant relaxed her hold on the head of the victim and with great resourcefulness suggested an aid to success. From a bit of rag produced from somewhere on her person she tore a narrow strip and wound it round the claws to reduce the gauge. The third attempt, however, produced no better result. With a further slight readjustment, the jaw of the weapon was then made to grip, and a few testing torsional preliminaries convinced the operator that only one final twist separated him from success. This was made with no uncertain design, and the seal of a completed task was evidenced in the triumphant manner in which the instrument flew from the seat of the trouble to the roof of Bob's mouth, where a sufficiently severe blow was delivered to divert the patient's attention from the former pain to a new one. Released from its padded vice, a tooth rolled across the floor towards the hearth, and a smile of satisfaction was noticeable on the faces of all concerned. The woman's big hands still held Bob's mouth open and she and her husband looked at their handiwork. Instinctively Bob's tongue wandered round his gums till it found the bleeding cavity, and lingering there for a moment or two, it passed on to the still unmoved, decayed tooth, which was standing as sentry over the yawning chasm that had so suddenly taken the place of its neighbouring denture.

There were too few resources of language and too little reserve of patience for Bob to do anything but snatch up his cap from the table and without consulting anyone about either fees or damages, he made his way back to his billet, cured of toothache, at least for a little while longer.[3]

---

3 As far as we know, Rider survived three years on the Western Front without a single battle wound.

Chapter 3

Two Sundays

Many terms came to have an entirely new connotation in the war atmosphere and among them was 'Rest Period'.

The deadening effects of a prolonged period in the trenches, under the cramping conditions of such limited space for operations, made it necessary to provide opportunities for more strenuous exercise. To go out for a 'rest' really meant for a period of vigorous activity, consisting of physical training, route marches and mock attacks.[1] Nevertheless, these occasions were welcomed as they afforded some acquaintance with village life, though often such villages were abandoned by all save billeted troops. They were far enough away from the front line to enable free movement with safety, except for an occasional long-distance shell or a short-lived aerial bombardment.

The battalion was quartered in one such village and the troops billeted in dilapidated barns, where the accommodation had already been claimed by the more permanent residents – the vermin and the rats. On the ground, once covered with new, clean, inviting straw, was about two inches of offensive dirty powder, the final form of the same straw after a hundred sections had trodden on it with muddy boots. This had become the veritable breeding-ground of large and small vermin, and these contested the right of any other living being to be in the barn. No comfort was possible until an organised attack had been made on at least the rodent class. Large, bold rats, interpreting the arrival of fresh troops as a new ration supply for themselves, early made their raids upon haversacks containing the 'unconsumed portion of the day's rations', and contestants

---

1 Describing the same rest period in the village that the account is about to indicate, Vaux-sur-Somme, Fairclough recorded that apart from battalion training, 'the companies in turn provided parties for repairing the lower road ... and digging sump holes to drain away the colossal quantities of mud' (Fairclough, p. 42).

chose to settle any dispute on the face or chest of the poor Tommy trying to make up his arrears of sleep.

Here and there in some villages, a family, perhaps through necessity, still tried to live on in the house adjoining the barn. The sight of a fire in the hearth lured Tommy to stand wistfully gazing through the doorway until the 'taken-for-granted' friendliness either expressed itself in an invitation to enter and share it, or – as was so often the case, and with some excuse – he was cursed and ordered away. But in his ignorance of the language he often interpreted the remarks as a welcome and still entered, only to be then pushed out. Temperamentally, Tommy was very different from the peasants in whose country he had been forced to dwell, and situations, both grave and gay, arose through his lack of appreciation of the other person's refusal to take the worst side of the war to heart.[2]

Sunday in a Rest Area was usually a drawn-out affair. If a Padre was with the battalion he was largely responsible for filling in the hours for the men with sit-around talks and arguments. In the earlier days, few chaplains were available and even the expected church parade was not forthcoming, with the result that men were left to themselves to fill in their Sunday leisure semi-alert hours. One man in the section, having no interest in discussions, had spent the evening in a village *estaminet*. After the men had drunk their evening tea, he came in rather excited and said – ' 'Eard the news, Corp.? Number Five Section's got the measles, and got it bad too. No one's allowed out of the village.' Most of the men had heard Tom's after-drink speeches many times before and knew what little value to put on them. Still, that was not the kind of thing he usually said, and there was a suspicion on the part of one man that this was more than a rumour. He stole out towards battalion headquarters and showed a greater keenness than usual in reading 'Orders', especially as the time for 'rest' was nearly up and another tour of the trenches was due.

Sure enough, the 'Orders' confirmed the news, adding that Number Four Section was also involved. The next morning, the whole battalion was placed in quarantine and movement even in the village was restricted, until every man had been medically inspected.

'How long does measles last? A six week's business ain't it, Corp.?'

'I think it is, but we can make good use of a nice spell like that here – don't you think?'

'You bet!'

2 The villagers were 'often bewildered spectators' of the British troops at sports, playing football and rugby (Fairclough, p. 43).

Days passed, and though no fresh cases of infection were reported the restrictions were maintained.[3] With little else to do, the men talked. A remark opened a discussion.

> 'This fight's a mug's game. I can't see how we are going to get much forrader carrying on like this.'
>> 'Aye! And I'd like to know whose b... scrap it is. It ain't mine, I know that.'
> 'Nor mine. I ain't got much interest in it neither. There ain't no bugles blowing out here, nor any pretty girls to pour out tea for yer, or singing to yer to let yer know how brave y'are to go out to fight. 'Eroes they call us; some 'eroes us! We ain't getting much out of it anyway.'
>> 'Nor anyone else, as far as I can see. When you've said all you can about soldiering and bravery and the like, this kind of war is not very sporting. What scope is there out here for showing what kind of a soldier you are? What's the good of 'cross-guns' on your sleeve if you don't see a blooming Boche from one week's end to another? It makes very little difference whether you are a bally General or a fool when it comes to stopping the kind of thing that's chucked about here.'
> 'When yer starts a thinkin' like, you wonder what yer doin' in this show at all. I've no grudge against any Fritz, I don't know any of them, and I don't see as how any of them can have a grudge against me as none of them knows me. I hate to think that I've anything to do with this b... business.'

He pointed to his bayonet.

> 'Why should I have to stick this into any man, be it the devil himself? I don't mind telling you, lads, that I hope it will never be my duty to do it. Where's the glory defending one's country in this b... way?'

The speaker warmed up to his subject and was surprised to hear his own words. Never before had he let himself go like that. He was about to apologise for his action, but was forestalled by the remarks of others who shared his ideas and who were anxious to add their contribution to what had been said.

---

3 The battalion was kept in quarantine (the infection being that of German measles), from 8 January to 10 March 1916 (Fairclough, p. xiv).

'And I bet Old Fritz won't feel any more pleased about it if he gets his spike in first. A fellow ain't got to be anti-British to admit that some of them are decent enough fellows. How about that sergeant we took back to the 'Cage' the other day, he who said he'd been a waiter in the Strand?[4] If he weren't over there in those trenches and didn't wear those clothes, who would be able to make an enemy of him?'

The Corporal was beginning to think that the conversation was running in a dangerous channel, and he sought in the excuse of going to Company Headquarters an early opportunity for arresting its progress. He felt a soothing reaction to his intervention, and knew his men well enough to know that allowing them to 'let off steam' would not affect their loyalty. After all, men, if they act as men, must have some private opinions about the things they are called upon to perform.

The rain was falling when darkness settled down on the village, and the men suggested continuing their 'pow-wow'. Having taken part in the afternoon's discussion, the Corporal felt under an obligation to attend and to use his influence to direct the discussion into a less dangerous path. Yet he wanted it to serve some useful purpose. The brazier gave welcome warmth and an air of friendliness to the gathering, and the conversation opened with his remark:

'I feel, lads, there's something wrong with things when, though we don't like having to do it, we cannot help being involved in a war like this. When I enlisted, I earnestly sought a way of establishing righteousness and peace. To me a sword or a bayonet seemed very unworthy instruments in such a noble enterprise. I would have used anything else that could have been found to do this, but I sought for it in vain. It's not that I am a coward but I don't like the business and I don't think we are hitting the right man when we strike. Nor does Fritz when he gets one of us.'

'We think that too, Corporal! But there's no other way, is there?'
'There's always been wars and I suppose there always will be', volunteered someone in the background.

'Let us hope not. I'm here because I've been persuaded that this is to be the last of wars.'

'A war to end war' came from a gentlemanly fellow who had been following the discussion with almost disturbing keenness.

4 The 'Cage' was the barbed-wire enclosure where prisoners were temporarily assembled and guarded.

The meeting continued, at first with enthusiasm, but it petered out when all the arguments that half-atrophied minds were capable of putting forth had been advanced. The proceedings ended in the inevitable singsong, except that into it crept one or two tunes that savoured of hymns and which had come to the surface through an association of ideas. The Corporal summed up.

'Look here, lads! We are in this business of the war now, and what we have been saying tonight must not make the slightest difference to our soldiering. We shall have our opportunity, I hope, after this show is over, and then we must all be "putting things straight again". That's a promise, is it?'

'It is, Corpr'l. It's when we get these damned rifles in our hands that by now our fingers glide instinctively to the trigger, and our eyes scan the horizon, almost in the hope that we can see a Boche to have a go at. We can't help it somehow. It's become second nature to us. When I drop it at the end of this show, I'll wash my hands of its pollution.'

This remark from a previously silent member almost re-opened the discussion, but the shrill sound of a whistle announcing 'Cook-house' broke up the party, and billy-cans were soon of more importance than arguments.

Another Sunday came round, and as though it had become an established rule, the company regrouped itself round the brazier anticipating a discussion on something or other. The conversation soon opened, and there was an early and amazing frankness and freedom which greatly impressed the Corporal. He, too, felt that it was an occasion for opening his heart, so he told them what he had never disclosed before – that at the outbreak of the war he was studying for the Church and was in college as a theological student.

'Well! You've got a different job now, anyhow, and a better one too, I reckon, Corporal!'

After a brief pause the speaker continued.

'It must be blooming hard work trying to preach religion these days. There's no place for the sob stuff now is there?'

'No!', said another, 'especially out here. One thing about it – we don't often get parsons here telling us chaps what we ought to do to be a decent fellow, 'cause the next minute we get an officer coming and telling us we've got to go over the top, and that means acting like a b... beast.'⁵

'It's not quite that bad surely. There is a bit of religion out here, don't you think?', said the Corporal.

But there was little conversation that evening and one by one the men wandered out.

When the next Sunday came, after the boredom of yet another routine week in quarantine, the men welcomed the opportunity of a pow-wow. 'Anything's better than sloggin' about in the mud of this God-forsaken 'ole!' – this was the approach of some men as they sat down. That night there came the unexpected suggestion that instead of a pow-wow they might have a real service. No Padre had been able to visit the unit for months, owing to the scarcity of chaplains, and an all-out service without one seemed unlikely. Said Tom –

'We've managed so far without one and I reckon the Corporal could give us a turn. It's in his line, ain't it?'

'What about it, Corporal?'

' 'Ear, 'ear! We'll rig you up with a nightshift and make a pulpit for you!'

These remarks showed that they were both eager and curious to see the Corporal in another role. Said another –

'And I bet he'll do a darned sight better than some of them I had to go and listen to at times.'

'Go on, Corporal, and we'll back you', was the promise from a few others.

The novelty of the scheme promised it having some support among the men, and the Corporal was persuaded to explore the possibilities. There were difficulties, however, not the least being getting permission from the battalion's commanding officers. There was another snag. No one else

---

5 The opinions of the speakers regarding their part in the war are not out of the range of the views one might have expected, although Rider may have been selective in noting those that he personally approved of, such as the dislike of having to kill and of crude incitement to hatred of the enemy. Nevertheless, it is perhaps unlikely that such views were expressed so early in the experience of the battalion, and more likely that they were expressed after the later disasters. In early 1916 the battalion had merely spent a short period in the trenches on a quiet front, where the physical conditions were dreadful but there was little enemy activity and hence few casualties. There appears to have been no occasion so far when any unit was required to 'go over the top' and 'act like a beast'. For further discussion, see the section on 'Attitudes' in the Introduction.

would approach the Adjutant, and yet for the Corporal to do so seemed presumptuous, as he was the one most involved in the favour to be requested. With many forebodings – through knowing the Adjutant's usual demeanour – he went to see him and braced himself to receive his reactions.

'A service? Um! Yes! Why not? But who's to take it?'
'I'm sorry, Sir. I have to speak for myself, but I ask you on behalf of the men.'
'Why you?'
'I was a preacher, Sir, when I enlisted.'
'That's interesting. You mean you were in the Church?'
'Yes, Sir. The Methodist Church.'
'Should you be given permission, where do you propose to hold the service?'
'Unofficially we have been having a kind of service in the barn at our billet, Sir.'
'Why are you not satisfied with that?'
'It's a very rough and ready affair, there is very little to create the atmosphere of worship, Sir, and the men have asked whether they could have an "All-out Service", with some music if possible.'
'That's unlikely, isn't it? Have you any idea where you are likely to find any musical instrument?'
'No, Sir. The only thing we know of is an old piano in the School.'
'But that's the Officers' Mess!'
'I know, Sir, and I was not asking for that.'[6]
'Well, go and see what you can fix up and come along to see me afterwards, Corporal. I'll speak to the C.O. about it. Wait, here he is now.'

The Adjutant took the Corporal to speak to the C.O., and the C.O.'s reception of the idea was that it would be a bit of a change for the men and quite harmless. This last fact he evidently was not too sure about, for when he did grant permission it was with the stipulation that the meeting be strictly religious and that a report be subsequently presented describing what took place.[7]

---

6 Chaplain Doundney recorded that at one 'barn service', when a piano was produced, a soldier who had answered a call for someone to play at the service and had been asked for a voluntary to introduce it, 'broke into Rachmaninov's "Prelude", and played it superbly' (Horne, *Doundney*, p. 144).
7 Perhaps this was the initiation of the report on Rider's pastoral activities which later persuaded the army to transfer him to a chaplaincy (Chapter 7).

The Corporal was naturally pleased with this initial success. He was still more so when the sanction had an official blessing, in the promise that notice of the service would appear in Saturday's Orders. When the Orders were published, they also included the statement that the service would be held in the Schoolroom. Although no officer was sufficiently interested to attend, yet there had been the decision to hand over the Officers' Mess for that hour.[8]

Twenty-five men supported the service, and when afterwards they were questioned by non-attenders on the matter of how the Corporal shaped, there seemed to be sufficient commendation to warrant a further trial. The Section being still in quarantine at the next weekend, it was an easy matter to repeat the arrangements of the previous Sunday, and a fifty per cent increase in attendance was encouraging. It was a simple service, without any of the aids to worship upon which one is inclined to depend. Without hymnbooks, singing was not an easy proposition as the memory of the new 'Pastor' was not too reliable. He 'lined' out the verses before each was to be sung, but most of the men were content to sing three times over the words they were sure of, leaving their more venturesome comrades to attempt to reproduce the suggested stanzas. The music also was somewhat uncertain and at times it seemed as though there were attempts at a descant.

In this second service there was a welcome new worshipper, in the form of a young officer who during the week had been drafted to the unit. He, reading the announcement about the service, decided to support it, fully expecting to find it in charge of a chaplain. When he realised that it was not the case, he was all the more interested and entered whole-heartedly into what took place. After the service, he encouraged the preacher and promised him to give him all the support he could when next he officiated.[9] All promises in the Army are provisional, so many are the eventualities that effect changes in plans. Before the next Sunday arrived, the battalion had received orders to proceed up the line to an unknown destination, and this order put the closure on the meetings, at least for the time being.

---

8 Rider must be exaggerating his success, since Fairclough noted that 'concerts were held in the schoolroom' (Fairclough, p. 42), although it may be that concerts were considered to be less likely to exclude members of the Officers' Mess than was a religious service, even one of only 'one hour'.

9 This remark links up with Chapter 5.

Chapter 4

In Action

A call to consolidate a position came, and a move up into the line was welcomed.[1] The destination was at first unknown, but the reasons for the move soon became clear, as every mile of the road gave an indication that big things were afoot. The mechanical and monotonous tramp along the cobbled roads was accompanied by a rumble as of distant thunder. When the men approached nearer to the line, the sound assumed more definition, and it was possible to sort out the heavy artillery fire from the more rapid fire of the field batteries. In confirmation of this, large guns were seen crouching in the semi-shelter of a sunken road, and the more mobile batteries of field guns were defying fate in open fields or at the sides of the roads. Troops were concentrating and appeared from all directions; everything pointed to operations on a grand scale.[2]

A welcome halt, made particularly agreeable by the serving of hot soup from the travelling kitchens, lasted only thirty minutes. Then the battalion divided into two sections and each proceeded independently to positions behind a small ridge of hills, where they halted until daylight faded into darkness and there was sufficient cover to enable the troops to move

---

1 Chapters 4 and 5 relate to the battalion's involvement in the 1916 Somme campaign, and in particular to the failed assault of 22–23 July on High Wood from Wood Lane. Although the battalion had served in trenches previously and had sent out parties into no-man's-land, with occasional casualties, this was its first participation in an over-the-top attack. For the majority of its existing members it was to be their first experience of this form of warfare, and for many their last. Despite the battalion being 'decimated', the survivors and reinforcements attacked again, on 30 July, with the same lack of success and the same slaughter. Elements of perhaps both actions are picked up in Rider's account. For the general picture, see note 16 of the Introduction.
2 'We found ourselves in the centre of bustle and excitement ... incessant streams of traffic passed both ways ... the artillery was continuously in action ... because we were new to this type of warfare, ignorance shielded us from too much anxiety ... although it is hard, after so many years, to describe the feelings of the moment, the impression remains that we were anxious to take our part in the great battle' (Fairclough, p. 57).

up into their new position. It was a piece of open country, and soon they were busy 'digging in'. Hard work with entrenching tools provided the men with small funk holes giving protection against rifle fire.

The men had been working with the handicap of an awful stench, making breathing a positive discomfort. The reason for this was not discovered until the first streaks of dawn enabled the men to see a little way ahead, to windward. Only a few yards separated the men from the carcasses of horses and the bodies of men which littered the ground, revealing the cost of an attempted cavalry charge of a few days before.[3] The sun rose in the heavens, but what the men had anticipated would bring them welcome warmth was now an agent in the rapid decomposition going on all around. Stray fragments of shrapnel shells pierced the blown bodies of the horses, ripping openings in them from which belched the most offensive gases, and these, carried on the light breeze, rendered the position unbelievably foul. There was no escape from the poisonous air and the mouth became dirty and dry, while the spitting made necessary was black and nasty, till the whole system heaved at the disgusting state of affairs.

Bad as conditions were, there was no alternative, at least for that day, so the men spent their time in trying to link up the line of funk holes to make them into a reasonable trench. Often in the attempt to do this a man would have to make a detour round the rotting body of an individual who, a few days before, had been given the same task. 'Oh 'ell!' came from the lips of a man who, being within range of an enemy whizz-bang, found his face all covered with what had been horseflesh. A well-placed shot had distributed the contents of a nearby carcass. Recovering himself later, he said:

> 'Bill! We seem to have struck an Eau-de-Cologne factory. I've 'eard tell as how France is noted for it. I shall have the pleasure of taking some of

---

3 'Great excitement was caused when the news came down that the cavalry had been in action at High Wood' (Fairclough, p. 57). It was fondly believed, as late as 1917, that a breakthrough in the enemy's trenched lines by the infantry would enable the cavalry to pass through and create massive disorder and panic behind the lines, as tanks were sometimes able to do in World War II, thus bringing the war to an end. (And, indeed, the momentary appearance of the cavalry on this occasion did briefly rattle the Germans, lest there had been a breakthrough: Miles, *Military Operations*, p. 89.) Hence, as A.J.P. Taylor remarked, gleefully and with perhaps some exaggeration, 'seven hundred thousand horses were kept in France throughout the war, waiting for the opportunity which never came, and using, for their forage, more shipping space than was lost to German submarines' (Taylor, *1914–1945*, p. 59). The cavalry action took place on 14 July (Taylor, *1914–1945*, p. 67); the battalion took up its position five days later. 'Another unpleasant feature of the sector was the number of dead horses, killed in the cavalry attack, which called aloud for burial' (Fairclough, p. 59).

it home to them as likes scent, for I'm due for leave tomorrow. It won't cost me much neither, for I feel blown up with it at present.'

But an envious pal commented:

'I shouldn't take that home if I were you, old man. They have got their share of troubles the same as we have.'

'It's a bally awful stink anyhow! Phew!'

And the speaker emphasised the fact by spitting frequently and dryly on the ground. The Corporal followed suit, involuntarily, endorsing what was said, but adding that we could 'thank God for a climate where the wind changes often'.

It was not until nightfall that there was any likelihood of finding a lee spot, and though the men dug hard all day they welcomed the order to abandon the trenches for a new position as soon as night began to fall. But the change of digs was not intended to give them better accommodation, only a better 'jumping off' place for a 'surprise' attack they were to make. It was so much a 'surprise do' that only fifteen minutes were to elapse before zero hour. However, it was to be only a little affair, just a make-belief as a preliminary to a greater show to follow a few hours later.[4]

It was suspected that three enemy machine-guns were established as outposts on the front that had been chosen for the attack, and since they were likely to cause a bit of trouble the Section had to 'mop them up' during their unexpected sortie on the enemy's position, before he had time to make use of them. To ensure success, no preliminary announcement of any kind was to be given of the attack, not even the customary artillery bombardment. The men were to creep out silently and take up positions as near to the enemy posts as they could, without being seen. Then, at a signal, all were to rush the positions simultaneously. Then they were to remain there as interested spectators of the 'big show'.[5]

---

4 The attack Rider is describing followed three earlier attacks by other troops in the same sector: the first on 1 July, with high casualties and no success; the second on 14 July, with inadequate success; and the third on 20 July, with again high casualties and no success (Carter, pp. 164–70). The 14th, with units of other regiments, attacked on 22 July.

5 Perhaps because this is an on-the-spot infantryman's view, the details of the overall intention and action are not wholly correct. Rider may also be misremembering. While the attack on 20 July was a 'surprise' one, inasmuch as there was no prolonged artillery barrage beforehand, the assault of the 14th on 22 July, beginning at 9.50 p.m., was preceded by six hours of barrage of the enemy positions in the sector – although in error the target of the 14th, High Wood, was missed (Carter, pp. 167, 177). The assault was intended, to some extent, to be a preliminary attack, as Rider states, and attention may well have been directed, at the level of the battalion and especially of the two companies first involved, to the silencing of enemy machine-guns.

At the signal to attack, up sprang the leading N.C.O.s. But as though they themselves had been responsible for it, there instantly followed a murderous enemy machine-gun fire which thinned out the ranks of the attackers almost before they had time to get on their feet. The survivors lay on the open ground, only a few yards from their starting point. The C.O., seeing what had happened, decided to send forward a part of the reserve company to support them. This also was unsuccessful, and the preliminaries to the great show were a hopeless failure. Fearing what might happen if the machine-guns were not disposed of, a further attempt to capture them was launched, but the advancing men were met with a still more murderous fusillade from what seemed to be innumerable machine-guns which broke up the attack as completely as each of the previous ones had been broken up. So far, every part of the scheme had misfired, and about fifty per cent of the battalion lay wounded and scattered on the ground in front.[6] Apparently it was impossible to alter the whole project at so late a stage in the operations, for there seemed to be no action on the part of Headquarters to modify the plan of campaign. Perhaps, thought the still surviving officer commanding the front-line operation, the telephone communications have broken down, a supposition confirmed by a report from the signallers later.

News of what had happened was then despatched by a runner, and the little group still in contact with the officer waited to hear what it was to do.[7] It seemed inevitable that the enemy would use the occasion of our failure to complete the disaster by launching a counter-attack. To meet this contingency, a 'strong-post' consisting of the officer, two signallers, a Company Sergeant-Major and one private, was established. They took up their position in a part of the old front-line trench, and each had to decide

---

6 The action proceeded as follows. It being dark, with no moon, two companies, A and B, left their front-line trenches and advanced, unnoticed by the enemy, through corn and towards the crest of a slight rise which separated the two sets of lines, 'lying down close to the enemy lines until the artillery fire lifted' (Carter, p. 178; Fairclough, p. 60). But the dash over the crest at 10.00 p.m., detected by the Germans partly by the light of flares, produced machine-gun fire which mowed the attackers down. Companies C and D repeated the assault, with the same result. There were so many similar disasters at the time that the official history dismisses this action in three sentences (Miles, *Military Operations*, pp. 136–7). Rider does not exaggerate the casualty rate.

7 Rider was correct. News of the annihilation of the first attackers only reached the C.O. one hour and twenty-five minutes later, by runner; and he had no telephone report until a further three hours later (Carter, pp. 179–80). Similarly, during the 30 July attack communications broke down, the telephone wires having been cut by shells, and pigeons and runners had to be used (Miles, *Military Operations*, pp. 165, 167).

between the alternatives of selling his life dearly or surrendering. Darkness was now beginning to settle on the scene and there was still no news from the return of the runner. All the men at the 'post' scrounged around for available extra munitions, and between them they managed to secure about six Mills bombs each,[8] which together with two revolvers represented their total military assets. Then in the quiet manner in which comrades act when faced with danger, without words they pledged themselves to each other and took their places shoulder to shoulder at the parapet of their new and official H.Q., to await their fate. A fifteen minutes' uncanny silence followed, made all the more intolerable by the deepening darkness and the fact that a few feet in front stood a field of standing corn. Not even a clearing had been made in the corn, except where, about ninety minutes before, the men setting out from that spot had trampled it down.

Suddenly the silence was broken by a sound that came with the firing of a salvo of enemy Verey lights. These flares began to fall almost on the strong-post, covering it with a blaze of revealing light, and revealing to those within how unpleasantly near the enemy positions were. The salvo meant but one thing to experienced soldiers, and without orders they stiffened themselves into steel, pulled out the pins from the Mills bombs in their hands, and resolutely faced the ordeal of the counter-attack. They knew that whatever was in store for them would not be long delayed. Commotion and noise followed the illuminations, and over no-man's-land came the party of raiding Germans, more eager to take prisoners than to kill. Every man in the 'post', grasping a bomb in each hand, peered into the black wall of corn, and for several minutes stood like tigers ready to spring. Then, with a suddenness equal to that with which it began, the raid came to an end and blackness shrouded everything as before, except that three less fortunate comrades in a post nearby had been snaffled by the raiders and were being hauled into their lines. But five grateful defenders, thanking God for their escape, were still alert.

The original zero hour for the opening of the main attack arrived, and the assault was launched according to plan, with the artillery putting down a heavy and continuous barrage on the enemy positions. On came the Scotties to their appointed objective.[9] They had not, of course, been informed

---

8 The Mills bomb, invented in 1915 by William Mills of Birmingham, was a hand-grenade whose explosive content was detonated by the automatic release of a spring lever four seconds after it was thrown.
9 The 'Scotties' were the King's Own Scottish Borderers, who were less successful than Rider implies (Miles, *Military Operations*, p. 137).

of the fate of the earlier assaults, and they were confused and surprised when they met, so early in their advance, living occupants in trenches they had expected to find vacated. In their confusion they stumbled over the bodies of the wounded men in the trenches. There was no time for deliberation, since the scheme of attack had been announced by the guns and already there was a murderous fire from the enemy machine-guns still in position. The Scotties, with the usual yell that announced the final stage of an assault, almost bulldozed their way across this shambles to their objective.[10] It was only sheer weight of numbers that carried the enemy positions and the 'mopping-up' was duly done, yet obviously not quite as planned.

A few of the preliminary attacking party, some of them wounded, had found their way back to the trenches from which they had sallied forth so hopefully a short while before. They were joined by a small number of men who had been in reserve during the attacks on the machine-gun nests. They grouped themselves to form a 'strong-point', in order to offer resistance to what was regarded as an inevitable enemy counter-attack. They received news that the Scotties had captured an enemy position and were holding it, and feeling fairly safe against immediate surprise attack they relaxed somewhat. Many of their comrades had fallen in front and were now between the Scotties and themselves, but were still under fire from the enemy reserve trenches.

Some of the group were now doing sentry duty in the forward trenches. They watched with a tenseness that imposed an almost unbearable strain upon their nerves. They longed for the dawn that would bring relief. Peering into the darkness, one of the group became suddenly alert, suspicious of movement in front. His observant eyes, made doubly keen by reason of their intensive scanning for nearly two hours, had certainly seen something. Slowly the movement continued towards the trench and the sentry, who stood still and silent at his post, picked out what looked like a crawling man. He became aware also of the movements of others. After a little while, one of the crawling figures called and made enquiries about the occupants of the trench. His answer came in the form of a rough handling which landed him at the bottom of the trench. Whoever it was that had accompanied him, if there had been another, had disappeared again into the darkness.

---

10 'Bulldoze' in the specific sense of moving earth, etc., came into use only in the 1930s, but in the more general sense of pushing through some action energetically, as here deployed, was in use much earlier (OED), hence this does not date the composition of this section of the account.

IN ACTION

The half-dazed man in the trench had sufficiently collected himself to answer the questions put to him by the sentries, and was soon put at ease when he was called by his name by a sentry who recognised him as one of the original party.

'Aye, lads, it's been hell out there. Boches and machine-guns in every d... place. Here! Tie up this bandage for me. I've stopped one in the leg.'

Sitting composedly on the firestep after having received attention, he continued his conversation.

'There's lots of poor devils lying out there in front, some not far away neither. They are lost. In the dark and in the confusion no one knows where he is, and I'm sure they don't know the way in. I'm mighty lucky to drop in here myself, for when I began to crawl I hadn't the faintest idea where I was until I came across you.'

The sentry again noticed movement and was less suspicious this time. Two figures loomed up in the darkness, for this time they came walking in. One was a machine-gun Corporal who, after handing over his companion, said: 'Here, lads, look after this fellow, he's got it in the shoulder.' No sooner had he said this than he again disappeared in the darkness in front.

A quarter of an hour later, at a point a little further along the line, a man was seen coming in on all fours, bearing another man astride his back. In response to a call for assistance, willing hands carefully lifted the second man, badly wounded, from the bearer. 'It's a bad one in the thigh he's got, lads! Be careful!' With that remark, the first man slipped away again into the night. Lookout men were alerted and reported that considerable movement was taking place just in front. Then, making their way in single file, came four men, each holding to the coat-tail of the man in front, the leader being confident of his direction and purpose. All were wounded, though less seriously than the previous survivors had been, but they were soon at home in the bottom of the trench.[11]

Their leader lingered on top until he saw that the three others were settled down. Then he said: 'I say, mates! There's one other fellow just out here who can't get in, and he's too hefty for me alone. He's got it in the

---

11 Fairclough tells a similar anecdote about a Sergeant Davis, who, on this occasion, although himself wounded, led back to the British lines some twenty wounded men, the whole party under fire, 'crawling on all fours' (Fairclough, p. 61).

back badly and he'll have to be carried. Will anyone give me a hand?' Without hesitation an offer was made, and jumping over the parapet the volunteer joined what he found to be the machine-gun Corporal.[12] Passing bodies which no longer needed human aid, together they crawled towards where the man lay about whom the Corporal was so concerned. In a shell hole, one which for the past two hours had done service as an advanced dressing-station for the wounded machine-gun section, the Corporal had collected his pals who had fared badly in the advance, and after attending to their wounds as best he could, had left them to console one another while he went out in search of the 'way in'. By arrangement, a password had been decided upon, it being the name of one of the party, Sam, and with this password each would be able to recognise the approach of any other. It had been used many times, for the occupants of the shell hole had been acting under the guidance of their Corporal. Only one wounded man remained there now. As he lay there, he wondered whether the same good fortune would be his as had been his pals'. He was listening intently for the password and it seemed so long delayed. 'Sh-s-s-h! He is here, mate, I think!', said the leading man in a hushed voice as he drew himself to the edge of a large hole.

'Sam!'

'Sam! Yes! Is that you, Corporal?'

'Aye! How are you feeling now, old man? D'ye think you can get in now? Shall we try again?'

'I've been trying on my own but I just can't move. I don't think you can manage. You had better leave me here. There'll be the chance of a stretcher party later, perhaps in the morning. You know where I am. I'm not feeling so bad now. You'd better be looking after yourself or you'll stop one in your own neck.'

'No! No! Come along now! Here's another pal to lend me a hand. Give us your arm!'

Between them the two bearers raised the wounded man far enough to get his arms round their necks. Supporting him thus, they were proceeding

---

12 If the dialogue that follows is trustworthy, the volunteer may possibly have been Rider himself. The volunteer says 'darned' in his report. Elsewhere officers and men say 'damn'/'damned', always written 'd...' (with one exception, Chapter 8, where it is spelled out), 'damn'/'damned' being swear words a pious Methodist of the time might have avoided saying or even repeating. There are, however, two instances where a soldier says 'darned' (Chapters 3, 15), although in one instance perhaps out of respect for Rider.

slowly in the dense darkness when a Verey light came soaring overhead and dropped almost at their feet, giving valuable information concerning the way. But it was meant for another purpose. The keen and searching eyes of the enemy had watched its flight and by its light they spotted a target. Instantly there followed the rat-tat-tat of a machine-gun, as it swept the area where movement had been observed. Down went the trio in a heap. A deep silence followed, broken later by a faint enquiry: 'Tom? Sam? Corporal?'[13]

Twenty minutes later a lone figure stole in from the direction of the enemy lines and, after having answered satisfactorily the challenge from one of its defenders, was allowed to enter the trench. He ambled along it in search of an officer and eventually came across a Captain who was the sole survivor among the men of commissioned rank.

> 'Darned hard lines, Sir! Corporal T... of the machine-gun section has had a bit of bad luck. All his men were hit as the first wave went over. He managed to get them all together into a shell hole, doctored them, and got five of them back. They are all along there, Sir! The other one, Old Sam, was badly hit, and the Corporal was carrying him in when he was "done in" himself. I'm not absolutely sure, Sir, but I think he's dead. He's only a few yards out in front, just over there.'

A couple of men were quickly on their way to the spot, bent on bringing in the luckless man. When the officer shone his flashlight on the Corporal, as he was being placed reverently on the firestep, a row of six bullet wounds across his back showed how well Fritz had done his job.

Corporal T...'s name never appeared in the Honours List; first-hand evidence of his bravery was not considered authentic enough.[14] Sam, who had been his pal for many months in the war, was still to be his companion, for they had 'crossed over' together and were to continue the next phase of their journey in one another's company, till they would give an account of what they had 'done in the Great War' to Him whose recognition of service is more generous and unerring.

---

13 To make sense of this story, it has to be understood that the new volunteer is calling out to the two who have been killed, that 'Tom' is the Corporal's name, and that he is called first by his name and then by his rank.
14 In the battalion's Roll of Honour, the only 'Corporal T...' reported dead in July 1916 is Lance-Corporal R.R. Tedstone, whose date of death is given as 23 July (Carter, p. 284), which fits. However, Rider may have chosen to conceal the name by not giving the correct initial. And Tedstone was not 'Tom' (previous note).

The remaining hours of the night were spent in collecting and tending the wounded, forgetful that the victorious enemy were only a few hundred yards away and in a very happy mood. So heavy had been the casualties that a part of the trench was reserved as a dressing-station till ambulance aid was forthcoming. When morning's light made evacuation work possible, it was not necessary for the bearers to spend much time there; a deep and peaceful sleep had come to many, and from it they could not be wakened.

Chapter 5

No-Man's-Land

Lying out in the open, isolated from his platoon and feeling hopelessly lost was one of the latest recruits. His battalion had suffered badly in an attack it had made upon enemy machine-gun positions. He was barely nineteen years of age and was where he was through his keenness to do his bit. There, in the dark on the open plain between his own and the enemy lines, he lay wondering what in the world he should do. It had been his first time in action and he was ignorant of anything to be done in an attack other than to obey orders. This he had done, and had accompanied his pals when they had advanced, and had got down when they got down. After a pause of several minutes he felt that he should be advancing again, but he could not find his pals and was too afraid to move or call. He at last decided that, if it was possible, he would make his way back again to the line from which he had set out, but where that was, he had not the faintest idea, everything being so dark. Verey lights were going up all around him, so it seemed, and he was unable to distinguish British lights from German ones. Growing more and more uneasy as the interminable minutes passed, he felt an irresistible desire to go anywhere rather than remain where he was. He set out half-aimlessly and many minutes later found himself at the edge of a field of standing corn. This encouraged him, for he recollected having passed such a place on his way out earlier in the night; but that it was the same field, or the same edge of it, he was not at all sure. To take it as a clue to direction he at first decided was unwise, but at a loss to know what else to do he took the risk, and forged along on his hands and knees.

Noticing something on the ground a little way in front of him and feeling half-afraid, he paused. It was motionless, and he decided to investigate more closely. Picking out the form of a body, he dared to call softly, but getting no response presumed that the man must be dead. He crawled still nearer, and though limited to his sense of touch he was able to assure himself that it was the body of a Britisher, a fact that enheartened him. Pushing ahead and leaving his pal, for this he had been to him for a while, though only a dead pal, he came across another similar form and again paused to watch. This time there was distinct movement and it was in the direction he himself was taking. Quickening his pace, he drew up almost alongside whoever it was and called softly:

'Hi there! Britisher?'
'Yes. Who are you?'
'Britisher! Do you know where the devil we are?'
'No! But it's from somewhere near here that we set out, I think. Come along! we'll get along together, lad!'

In response to this welcome invitation, he joined the other, but the progress was terribly slow, his new pal finding the going very difficult.

'Can't you get along quicker, old man? Are you hurt?'
'I am, lad, but we cannot have far to go now.'
'Let me give you a hand. Where are you?'

Feeling around in the dark, he grasped the man by the shoulder strap and his fingers traced out the single star on it which denoted that his comrade was a subaltern.

'You're an officer, aren't you, Sir?'
'Yes.'
'Come on then, Sir, let's stand up and walk it.'
'I'm sorry, lad, but I cannot hurry. I'm nearly done in.'

Following this up with a remark in a weaker tone, he said:

'You get along yourself, don't trouble about me, I'll get in later if I can.'
'No, Sir, I am not going to leave you here on your own.'
'You must. If you can remember where I am, you perhaps will be able to send out a stretcher for me.'
'I'll bring one myself, if I can, Sir.'

Reluctantly he prepared to go, but was delayed a moment by a question from his pal:

'Do you know Corporal J...?'
'No, Sir.'
'He's in the Signal Section.'
'I've been in the regiment only since last Friday, Sir. But what about 'im? I'll find 'im, if it's 'im you want, Sir!'

In slower and fainter tones the enquiry was followed up with a request:

'If you happen to see him, tell him where I am and that I should like to see him here, if he can get to me.'

'I'll tell 'im, Sir! But who are you? Who shall I say wants to see 'im?'

'Lieutenant H... .[1] Get on in, lad, you won't have far to go, I think. Good luck to you.'

'Are you sure you can't come too? 'Ere, let's have another try, Sir.'

This sincere gesture was graciously declined with the words:

'Thank you, lad ... But I'm nearly finished ... Leave me ...'

Slowly at first, as if it were a cowardly thing to do, the lad stole away with the half-smothered benediction: 'Gawd bless you, Sir.' Crawling only twenty yards, he reached the other edge of the standing corn and saw where it had been trampled down in the immediate front of the trenches. He boldly attempted to cross these few yards and was challenged in English. Though he was startled and somewhat nervous, he was profoundly thankful for those words and nearly lost his life through not answering them satisfactorily. He threw himself into the trench and it was a few seconds before he could speak coherently enough to make his identity and business known. Recovering from a mild cursing he had received through his folly, he busied himself with his commission from the man he had left in no-man's-land.

Good fortune favoured him, and in ten minutes he had traced the Corporal and was attempting to state his business:

'Corporal, I ... er ... you ...'

'Well, get on with it, lad! Pull yourself together!'

'That new officer that joined us last week, H... he says he's called, 'e's badly wounded and 'e's only just out there, and 'e says 'e wants to see you, if you can go.'

'Who says so?'

' 'E told me 'imself, Corporal. I've only just left 'im. 'E says 'e's done for. But 'e specially asked me to let you know 'e wanted to see you.'

---

1 'Lieutenant H...', who presumably died on 23 July, cannot be identified from the battalion's Roll of Honour. A Second-Lieutenant S.H.P. Hewett is reported to have died on 22 July, a Lieutenant F.P. Hodes on 24 July, but there are no other H... names of officers who died during either the July or the later September attacks (Carter, p. 281). However, the reported dates may not always be exactly correct. On the other hand, as with 'Corporal T...' (previous note), Rider may have chosen not to give the correct initial.

There was a brief pause during which both men were thinking hard. Then the recruit said: 'Come along, I'll take you to 'im myself.' Soon he had mounted the parapet and was making his way towards where the officer had been left, and with the Corporal at his heels the twenty yards were quickly covered. 'Sh! ... Sh! Sh! Listen! ... Sir! Is that you?' Only a very feeble response came. Then pulling the Corporal by his sleeve, he pointed a few feet in front, saying: 'There 'e is!' 'Thank you', said the Corporal, 'you had better get back now.' The Corporal drew himself alongside the wounded officer and offered his services. There was no reply.

'Sir! You are Lieutenant H... I believe. I am sorry you are hit.'

'Is that you, Corporal?'

'Yes, Sir! What can I do for you? Let me try to get you in first, you are only a very short way out.'

'It's no use, Corporal, some other good fellow has tried but I'm done!'

Then he drew his limp arm slowly over his chest and bringing it to rest over his breast pocket, said with an effort:

'I haven't had ... a chance ... of doing ... much ... out here ... and for you ...'

'That's not your fault, Sir! You've done all you could do.'

'Take this ... little book ... here from my ... pocket ... You will find my address there ... write to ... my ... father ... tell him ... a ... what you know. Say ... I ... I ... I ...'

The sentence, if it was completed, was heard only in the Great Beyond. The Corporal lingered for a while, but knowing that his services were no longer required, breathed silently over his body: 'Into Thy hands, O God.'

With his precious token of trust, the Corporal made his way back again to the front line, hearing the echo of words he had heard just a few days before in a little village school:[2] –

'You can rely on my support, Corporal, in what you are doing for these men.'

---

2 See Chapter 3. But Rider is telescoping, for effect. The battalion left the rest area on 10 March (Fairclough, p. 43), a Friday, and the previous Sunday was 4 March. Lieutenant H... died on 23 July, some four months later, not 'a few days'. In between the battalion had served on the Arras front, but no action there seems to fit the circumstances described ('an attack upon enemy machine-gun positions'), circumstances which do fit the July action on the Somme. Nor, for what the argument is worth, was any 'Lieutenant H...' of the 14th killed on the Arras front.

1 *Robert J. Rider photographed in his army chaplain's uniform during World War II.*

2 Pencil drawing by Rider, entitled 'Consecrated Ground, Rocklingcourt Church'. The drawing is dated 1916 and so was presumably composed while Rider was serving in France.

PLATES

3 Pencil drawing by Rider, entitled 'Our Home from Home' and probably dating from the same time as the previous illustration.

PLATES

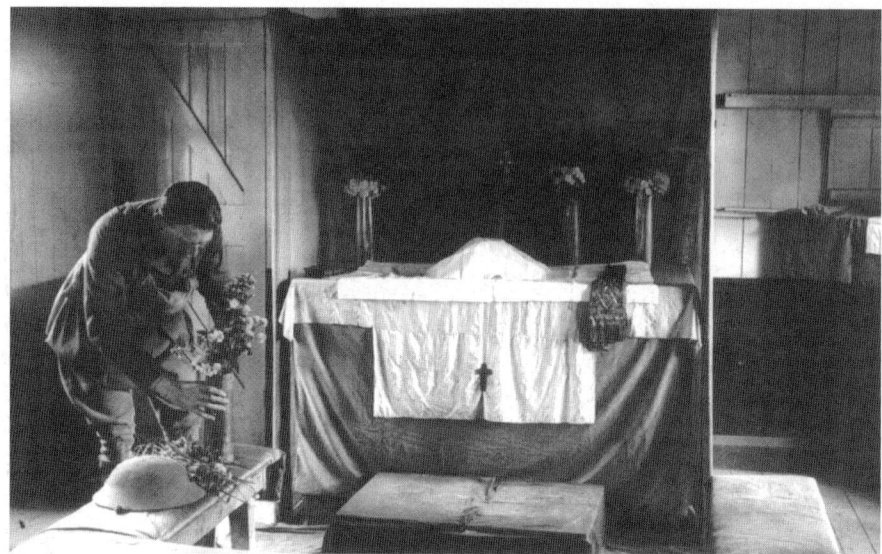

4 *An army chaplain decorating an altar in a church hut at Sailly-Labourse, 4 June 1918. (IWM Q11041)*

5 *Chaplains of the English Presbyterian and Dutch churches conducting the South Africa Brigade's memorial service at Delville Wood, 17 February 1918. (IWM Q10673)*

6 *A chaplain writing a field postcard for a wounded man, July 1916. (IWM Q4060)*

7 *An advanced dressing-station on the Somme battlefront, September 1916. (IWM CO754)*

8 *German prisoners of war carrying stores during the Battle of Arras, 9 April 1917. (IWM Q5180)*

9 *Retrieving the pay book from a dead soldier for identification. (IWM Q23562)*

PLATES

10 *One of the photographs Rider brought back from France, entitled 'Home Again, Belgium'.*

11 *An army chaplain assisting an elderly refugee, Bethune, 11 April 1918. (IWM Q10888)*

PLATES

12 *Sorting out the packs of the dead and wounded so that personal effects could be sent home, Guillemont, September 1916. (IWM Q4245)*

Chapter 6

Fear Overcome

Normal rest periods were undergoing a change.[1] The customary 'loosening' exercises for men who had been cramped in trench life gave place to a new form of training. The 'Tactics of an Advance' were new features and were in contrast to those of defence with which men had become so familiar. Also the training was intensive, which suggested that new plans were being made for the future. The men in one way welcomed the change. To be a part of an army on the move seemed almost too good to be true after the dull monotony of the past two years of stagnant warfare. Some old hands, however, were not so keen on movement which was to bring them into closer contact with the enemy.

Aerial reconnaissance work had given the staff such complete information about the enemy trench system that, in every detail, replicas of the positions were made in the training areas. Each unit practised again and again in sham warfare what was to be its serious duty some time in the near future. This was done both by night and by day, so that when the time arrived the men would be able automatically to perform what was expected of them. Every section of 'specialists' was to be employed; bombers for this task, machine-gunners for that, scouts for a particular job, and signallers were brought to a standard of efficiency that betokened great responsibilities. The distribution of a number of new weapons of attack – ugly-looking knives, special bombs for storming dugouts – all indicated desperate close-up work in places where both rifle and bayonet were unsuitable.

---

1 The final section of this chapter relates to August 1916, and the middle section requires no specific date. The opening section, when at first it deals with the preparations for action, seems to relate to the training for the Somme campaign, enlarging on the early part of Chapter 4. But when the section goes on to refer to past battle failures and the 'fortunate survivors', this seems to point back to the July 1916 battles – Rider had left the battalion before the September battles. The 'rest period' between these battles, in August, seems much too short for the training described, and we conclude that the first section is confused chronologically.

Those men who had known battle before, and had experienced failure and knew what it cost in human sacrifice, did not anticipate with any relish the opportunity to be given them for translating their intensive training into action. The usual enthusiasm with which a change of operations was greeted was absent. When the order came to move up into the line, it was acknowledged with a cheer that was more the liberation of pent-up feelings than a mark of keenness. The whole scheme was entirely void of attractiveness, and only the fact that it was to be another dose of unquestioned duty gave a man the heart to do his best.

The personnel of the old battalion had so completely changed, since it had been called upon so often to take part in a scrap, that the fortunate survivors of the original crowd were looked upon by the recruits as battle-scarred veterans and were given a certain amount of respect. The new men invited them to recount their experiences, and were very anxious to know whether men got 'all worked up' when they went into a battle. There was a positive abhorrence of the idea of being in a bayonet charge where they were to do some deliberate killing. It seemed so different from 'accidental' killing with shells or bombs, or killing from a distance as when men were shot.

★★★

Only an hour was left before an attack was to be made. Detailed instructions were issued to all concerned and the officers gave a few words of counsel and cheer to their men to brace them up for their task. The Signals Corporal found himself faced with a real problem. One of the oldest of his men, a man who had been with him through most of the previous 'shows', was exhibiting signs of battle-fear. It was the result of a strange presentiment the man had experienced, a presentiment which so often came to men and to which they attached great significance. He was obviously under a severe nervous strain; great beads of perspiration stood out on his brow and he moved about restlessly, though only within the very limited confines of his dugout. Such conduct was very disturbing, especially at that hour, as there were only a few minutes in which to detail the work. The Corporal, too busy just then to give this man any special consideration and hoping that, before he returned from posting the other signallers, he would have got over it, left him alone.

When he returned, the man was crouching in his funk hole and was as difficult to move as a limpet from a rock. The military way of dealing with such a behaviour was drastic and relentless. The Corporal shrank from going that way to work, yet felt he was faced with a situation that was demanding enough for a full-blooded chaplain and much too stiff a proposition for him. Breathing a prayer to God, he returned to the man and was about to deal with him when the senior officer came along the trench. The Corporal thought the matter would now be taken out of his hands, but almost accidentally he screened the man with his body. The officer fulfilled his duties without having noticed what was taking place, and went on to the next 'post' with: 'Well, good luck, Corporal!'

The preliminary bombardment had already begun and the men were alert, all except the signaller who was still terror-stricken. Knowing that bullying tactics would fail, the N.C.O. got down alongside the man and placing his hand on his shoulder said: 'Now Frank! In a few minutes your fellow men will be depending on you. You are not the sort to betray them.' Still no response. 'This is a case, man, where God comes in. Give Him His opportunity to help you to play the man. He'll do it. Now how about it?' Immediately, as though helped by an unseen hand, the man roused himself and went boldly to his tasks. In a few minutes he was sallying forth with the first wave in the attack, laying out a wire to establish communication between the headquarters and the assaulting force. All night he worked fearlessly and took many unnecessary risks with an incomparable courage.

Early next day, when the fighting had died down and the troops were busy consolidating their position, the Corporal sought out the signaller and unostentatiously congratulated him on his fine work during the attack. It was indeed fine work, for overcoming his own fears was a far greater achievement than overcoming the enemy. His victory had not been an easy one, and he was still under nervous strain when he heard the encouraging words of his N.C.O. They proved to be too much for him. Leaning on the Corporal's shoulder, his reaction expressed itself in copious tears, representing the last stage in a battle he had fought and won. One should not look for bravery in callous men. It is seen in men who first know fear. This was not the last time that the signaller gave 'God an opportunity' in his affairs. A few successful experiments resulted in the establishment in his life of a definite confidence in Him, which he openly acknowledged.

★★★

That spell in the battle-line ended, and when the unit was out at rest news came to the Corporal that he had been granted a Commission as a Chaplain to the Forces.² It was with very mixed feelings that he received the news and later said farewell to his old pals, but he was encouraged by the fact that they shared the disappointment with him. As he moved off to the railhead, en route to England, his problem man said: 'Good luck! Try and get back with us, Corporal!' But strong emotion forbade any promise to do so. He did return to the battlefield, but not to his old infantry regiment; it was to an entirely new department of the fighting machine, the field artillery, where most things were strange to him.

---

2 For Rider's translation to a chaplaincy, see the Introduction.

Chapter 7

Problems of a Padre

The War Office, knowing the handicap of having many too few Chaplains to the Forces, and feeling also that the sources of supply of new Chaplains were drying up, decided to offer Chaplaincies to qualified ministers and clergy, then serving as combatants.[1] One of these appointments was offered to the Corporal, on whose voluntary work a report had already been made. It was assumed that a change from the ranks to commissioned ranks, and into a specialist department, the R.A. Corps of Chaplains Department,[2] was just as easy a transition as being posted to a new regiment.

The raw Chaplain's early reactions to his new post were not very pleasant. Two years in the ranks had almost killed initiative in action and originality in thought. He felt mentally dull, and shrank from having to take up any position of leadership. He sadly missed his old pals and their chumminess which had meant so much to him. He felt shy at the altered relationships between the men and himself and between the officers and himself; he was conscious of a clumsy amateurishness in most of his work. As a slight compensation, he enjoyed a new freedom of action, yet with it he did not feel he was able to get as near to men as when he shared bed and board with them in the ranks.

As a ranker, he had never felt within measurable distance of a Regimental Sergeant-Major, and he was startled by the recognition from one when, on the very first day, the R.S.M. of his own unit greeted him with a fine smart salute and clicking of heels. His feelings were something like men must have when they are being knighted by His Majesty the King at Buckingham Palace.[3]

---

1 On this development, see the Introduction.
2 More correctly, the Army Chaplains' Department.
3 This must have been written before 1952 when a female monarch succeeded the three previous kings who had reigned during or after World War I.

He had a great deal to learn about that part of the personnel of a unit that seems so remote from the ranker – the officers. In their mess he was introduced to a new form of camaraderie, which turned out to be as real and brotherly as anything he had known in the ranks. Man's heart undergoes no change when the man dons a new uniform. There are common factors of friendship in every place where men have to work and live together, and there is the universal need for, and practice of, comradeship.

Among guns and ammunition limbers an old rifleman feels strange. The Padre, without previous experience and almost without having had any contact whatever with a Padre of any kind, was perplexed about his duties, and not having received any information about what was expected of him he had to plough his own furrow. No one took over a position with less to guide him than did a chaplain in those days. It was difficult to decide whether a Padre was a part of the Army or only attached to it – whether with honorary rank he was really an officer, or just shown the courtesies of rank by fellow members of the mess. The only counsel given relating to his work came in the form of a casual remark heard in the process of 'posting', and in the formal style of Army Orders, 'the Rev. ... is posted to you and is responsible for the spiritual guidance of the troops'. When, how, or where, were matters still to receive consideration, for all guidance on such matters was at that point entirely absent.

In the early days of exploring the possibilities of the situation, a pleasant interlude occurred which temporarily relieved the anxiety. One of the privileges of being with an artillery unit was that the officers were allowed a 'mount', called by them a 'charger'.[4] Such a privilege was an agreeable surprise to one who had known all the rigours of two years 'foot-slogging', and it was accepted by him as one of the compensations for the losses in other ways. The Padre was escorted to the horse lines to interview the Sergeant-Major, in order to be 'fixed up'. The S.M. was one of sufficiently long-standing to have acquired a complete knowledge of the routine and tactics of every department of Army work. Apparently anxious to do his best for the new Padre, he promised to see that he was 'fixed up with something suitable'. He even volunteered the suggestion that the Padre had better try some of the horses for himself and decide which one suited his particular style of riding. It may be observed in passing that it is not the custom to leave good mounts orphaned in the Army, and any unplaced animal is suspect.

---

4 Even in the infantry, senior officers rode horses, and supplies were pulled by horses, so that 'an infantry division had 5,600 horses to its 18,000 men' (Taylor, *1914-1945*, p. 8).

Among the 'possibles' there were many specimens of horseflesh which were presumably attached to the battery for rations only. One or two of these were given a place in the 'March past' on this occasion. Grooms were doing their grooming automatically, their eyes being in the direction of the trial, for, knowing the horses, they were interested to know what being 'nicely fixed up' meant. Past experience had taught the Padre more about sergeant-majors than about horses and he felt convinced that this was a time when he should trust experience and move cautiously. Pointing to a certain horse, the S.M. singled it out as one he felt he could recommend – on what grounds he did not say. Instinct warned off the prospective horseman, whose past experience had not included horse riding in any other form than an occasional trot on a superannuated beast doing duty at the seaside. He side-tracked the S.M. by suggesting that 'number three horse' took his fancy more. He knew he would have to face the ordeal of making his debut as a jockey and that he was to have a critical and curious audience to wish him 'bon voyage'. He therefore decided to get it over as soon as possible. He mounted the 'probable', anticipating the worst, and gave a display that evoked the sympathy of a courteous officer who had been in the offing, and having until then considered it infra dig to make any suggestion. Convinced that a little advice would not be presumptuous, the officer suggested that the matter could be decided later, a very welcome proposal which was accepted with profound though unostentatious gratitude. It had, however, come too late to leave the Padre with any prestige as a horseman.

Later, from the 'spares', one horse was promoted to the position of 'officer's charger'. But even in that dignified estate it was incapable of abandoning all its idiosyncrasies at a moment's notice, or of behaving with at least some suggestion of appreciation. One of its special dislikes was to have anything within yards of its hind-quarters, and when this inadvertently happened it would land out with both hind feet, simultaneously, in the direction of the intruder. The S.M. was fully acquainted with this weakness, as he was of the vices and virtues of every horse in the lines under his care. A few days later, the battery was on the move, with the Padre riding moderately safely on his horse, in a place of honour at the side of the Battery Commander and thus at the head of the column. The S.M., in forgetfulness (perhaps), allowed his own horse to approach from behind as far as a nicely calculated position of safety for himself – a deliberate invitation to the Padre's mount to perform. Without the slightest warning, the beast lashed out and flung itself into the air, all four feet being off the ground at once, completely unseating the rider. He, with tattered dignity, fell in a heap, in front of his mount, after having given it a prolonged and affectionate embrace with both arms round its neck. In that position, the eyes of the horse met those of the Padre and there seemed to be a sort of sympathetic understanding between them. For already there had been established a sufficiently strong friendship between them which, had it been possible, would have avoided such a contretemps.

In addition to this weakness, 'Jimmy' (as the horse was called), had a mouth as hard as the Rock of Gibraltar. More often than not the direction taken was in the nature of a compromise between the desire of the rider and the whim of the ridden. 'Fixed-up' the Padre certainly was, and being that much better equipped for his work, he settled down to take up the more serious part of his duty.

It happened that a Padre colleague had gone down the line sick, and had passed on his duties to him, and through this arrangement he was to renew his acquaintance with the trenches. Soon after dinner one day, he made his way into the line, and it being a quiet day, many of the troops had relaxed and were ready for anything out of the ordinary routine. Since it was a relatively unbattled sector, the Padre considered the possibilities of a short service. There was nothing ecclesiastical about this induction service. A sand-bagged section of the reserve line trench was the chancel; the firestep did duty as altar and pulpit combined. The only musical accompaniment was the scream of the high-velocity shells and the droning tones of the larger shells tearing their way towards some unfortunate billet in the rear. The sermon was interrupted by the occasional 'rat-tat-tat' of the enemy machine-guns as they swept the parapets for any incautious sentries. Once there was an instinctive pause in the proceeding occasioned by the familiar sound of an approaching 'heavy', and every man crouched down in the trench, awaiting the explosion which came and faded away without causing any casualty.

The men welcomed the service both for its novelty and for the 'change' it brought.[5] Conducting religious services had other risks. One particular Sunday evening a voluntary service was arranged in the waggon lines. The only covered place available as a sanctuary was a large hole about twelve feet square and three feet deep, covered with a large tarpaulin supported along the middle by a pole placed so as to give just sufficient head-

---

5   Rider is reminding the reader that his former CO had thought that a religious service would be 'a change for the men' (Chapter 3).

room for a man standing there. At a push, the place would accommodate twenty men.

By this time there were officers in the mess who had shown some interest in the Padre's work, and some of them intimated their willingness to support his services in the 'bivvy' on a certain condition: that they had one all to themselves. In their judgement, it was not in the best interests of 'His Majesty's Service' to have to share such limited accommodation with the rank and file. Any suggestion of relaxing the strict discipline of the Army on active service was considered unwise, and hence to have to 'squeeze in' with the men in such intimacy was undesirable. Also, there was the suggestion that such a meeting would put restraint upon the free expression of the men's emotions and exchange of ideas. The Padre sensed the real nature of the condition, and though it involved a compromise with some of his religious ideas, he felt that it could be justified under the circumstances. At any rate, it was too good an opportunity to be missed. It is extremely difficult to get one hundred per cent Christianity anywhere; it is often wise to accept just what little there is, in order to provide the taking-off ground for something better. Arrangements were therefore made for two services, one for the men and another for the officers. Because of the special consideration given to them, the latter turned up in full strength, supported by the Colonel himself. This arrangement held good until fate decided it should terminate.

On one particularly lovely Sunday evening, after a meal which had followed the evening service, eight officers and the Padre were enjoying a smoke outside the bivouac. It was a peaceful scene in the fading glory of the sinking sun, which was tinting everything with the after-glow of sunset. Conversation was light and appropriately happy. An aeroplane made its way overhead at a low altitude but attracted little attention. As it was making its way in the direction of the aerodrome about three miles back, it was assumed to be an English plane returning from a successful reconnaissance flight over the enemy lines. But in a few minutes it came back, and silently volplaning from the skies into a position of advantage, it dropped a large bomb, which fell, with deadly accuracy, within five yards of the group of officers. Down went the entire party. When the smoke and dirt had cleared, the half-stunned survivors tried to ascertain what had happened. Three did not rise at all, and were never found. Four others were able to stir themselves only enough to note their wounds and to call for assistance. The only untouched member of the party was the Padre, who, though shaken, was called upon for immediate intensive work. This enemy success was a clever and daring bit of work on the part of an aviator who, selecting the last shadows of evening as cover, made a 'dash-and-run' raid on our position.

The C.O. had been absent that evening from the service as he had gone off, for a few hours, to a town some miles behind the lines, to enjoy a brief respite. Long after dark he returned, and it was the Padre's unpleasant duty to inform him of what had happened in his absence. The two of them went over to the bivvy, which a few hours before had been a sanctuary but which now was doing duty as a mortuary. Returning to the Colonel's dugout, they spent much of that night together, and there was a call for the ministry of consolation. When the Battery Commander drew up the official report, the Padre was the sole available witness of what had happened. It was under deep emotional stress that the report was written. 'Old Byron gone! Poor devil! – the finest chap this regiment will ever have!' In the conversation that followed, the Padre tried to cheer the officer by suggesting that the fact that he was absent from the camp at the time of the 'trouble' had been providential, and that thanksgiving to God would be appropriate.

> 'This tragedy, Colonel, was perhaps not staged by Providence, but it can be used by Providence. We shall see, Sir!'
>
> 'I suppose, Padre, I'm a lucky dog, but I really cannot see how God can have had anything to do with it. A "stolen respite" is scarcely providential. Even if it were, I reckon He's made a d... poor selection to single me out for the distinction.'[6]

Tarrying sleep gave the Padre time for thought. He wondered whether having separated the officers from the men indicated a dilution of the faith he had had when he first began soldiering. It was not the only compromise in morals that he had sanctioned of late, and he was troubled.[7] Then, too, there was the unfortunate fact that the only casualties that evening had been among those officers who a few minutes before had been keen enough to worship.[8] That unfortunate bombing raid decided the fate of the services. The new officers who had been sent as reinforcements were to have their baptism of fire in the line before they would have

---

6 The account is honest in that the Colonel comes off better in the exchange.
7 See note 54 of the Introduction.
8 Rider chastises himself (and questions providence) too harshly. The group of officers was bombed, not at the service but later, apparently following the conclusion of a meal together, and therefore after a gap of more than just 'a few minutes'.

the opportunity of worshipping together, and conditions were never favourable again.

The unofficial side of the Chaplain's work was the limit of his activities for some time to come. He was grateful, however, for his experience as a ranker in the trenches, for through it he had learned much about dangers and how both to assess them and to avoid them. Using sound sense, it was possible to face stern ordeals calmly, and by so doing to make it easy for others of less experience to do the same. Chaplaincy work in the field is really Comradeship.

Chapter 8

Blood and Fire

'Hullo, Padre! Great morning this! What's the news?' This was the greeting he received one beautiful morning on his arrival at the waggon lines. 'Everything O.K., Mac![1] The same here, I hope?' 'Yes, thanks!' Drawing attention to a new officer standing nearby, the C.O. introduced him with the remark:

> 'This is Woods, Padre. He has just joined us. The lucky blighter left London only the day before yesterday. If you are going back to the guns, you might take him up with you and introduce him to the C.O.'
> 'With pleasure! I shall be ready in about an hour, Woods.'

In the interval, the Padre made a routine call at the waggon positions and spoke to the men and officers. Friendly chats with the latter were very revealing, as mention was made of the merits and demerits of individual men whose part in some unusual event in the life of the unit gave them the right to special mention. Enjoyment was often found in the use of the privilege of recording the *faux pas* of some unsuspecting fellow who had 'let himself in for it', the news being retailed solely that the ministry of humour might be deepened. Ungrudging praise was generously given when commendation was deserved, and even when the misdoings of men came under review it was invariably in the interests of the men themselves. Often too when the praises of men were being sung the loudest, they themselves would be least conscious of it, as the confidential conversation that follows might well indicate. One officer said –

> 'By the way, Padre, that new Bombardier who joined us from the other brigade a few weeks ago – you asked me to give him a sympathetic and understanding trial in the battery – he seems a jolly decent sort.[2] He's

---

1 The account later calls another officer 'Mac', presumably in error.
2 'Bombardier': the title of a soldier in the artillery.

got a rare hold on his section already. Do you know anything more about him?'

'I do. Quite a lot.'

'What?'

'I don't know, Mac, whether what I know is much in your line. But it's an interesting story and is worth hearing – if you would like to hear it. We don't all understand our fellows, and some would misinterpret incidents in the lives of others which happen to be a bit out-of-the-ordinary. So if I tell you, it will not be for general retailing.'

'I'm interested, Padre. Get on with it.'

★★★

Well, in civil life the Bombardier was a Salvationalist, and this fact was soon known to his pals after he joined up. He is a real good fellow whose sterling qualities need no advertisement, and he has a knack of getting on with everyone. With him in his last battery there was a terror of a fellow, nicknamed Badger, whose conduct seemed to confirm the rumour that he had been a professional burglar and had been in gaol more than once. Competing with this reputation was the even more damaging one of being able to tell lies with a shamefacedness that was almost unbelievable. Then, too, he had an ungovernable temper which at times made him like a wild beast. Poor beggar, the product of a rotten upbringing in a drunken home in a city slum, he had had to make his way in surroundings where every vice was a commonplace. But he was as good a soldier as he was a liar and scrounger, a fact that spared him many a merited punishment. In sheer despair, Commanding Officers had 'shunted' him on to other batteries till he landed in D Section. Well, using the Bombardier's own words: 'I'm going to experiment on him with the Grace of God'. This he carried out by taking a special interest in Badger, often giving the impression that it was by accident that they were placed together in the same billet. After-duty hours were also given up to Badger, yet never a word said to him in the old way about religion. A strong bond of friendship sprang up between them, and the quiet influence of the Bombardier's character began to tell on Badger. There was, in addition, the factor of the Bombardier's intercessions on Badger's behalf. Well, to cut a long story short, this happened.

One morning when Badger could not find his cardigan, the Bombardier offered to lend him one of his own, and it was a Salvation Army cardigan. The Badger accepted the offer. It turned out to be an unexpectedly hot summer morning, and when all the men were in the lines grooming their horses, the officer in charge gave the orders: 'Coats off!', followed by 'Tunics off!' As soon as these orders were obeyed, a round of suppressed laughter came from all the men present. Badger was wearing a scarlet cardigan with the 'Blood and Fire' emblem on it![3] Patently the incorrigible thief had stolen the Bombardier's jersey! The wearer tried to carry off the situation as though he was not aware that the merriment had any association with him, until he could no longer pretend otherwise because of the many loud comments and witticisms directed at him. Yet there was an unusual quietness and lack of aggressive response on the part of Badger, and this so impressed one of his chums standing nearby that he came to realise that Badger was not treating the revelation as merely a joke on himself. Turning to him, he half-whispered: 'Say, Badger! Yer ain't serious, are yer?' A nod of assent furnished the reply, and an awkwardness on Badger's part confirmed it. The Bombardier had been successful with his experiment, but had had the wisdom not to call upon Badger for the usual form of witness-bearing, indicating that a change of heart had taken place.[4]

★★★

The officer had listened attentively.

'Well I'm d...! And what happened then?'
'The joking continued even when the truth was out. To many of the men the change of attitude was a bit of silly sentimentality. Others were careful, since they had reasons for not taking risks with Badger. They were not sure whether his temper and his punch had been in any way affected by the 'Grace of God', and they exercised a reasonable restraint upon their wit. That's the position at present. It's been a rather long story, Mac! But you know now why the Bombardier is respected and why conditions in the section are altered.'
'It's a most unusual story, Padre. I've always held that war drives a man to the Devil; I've never known it drive him the opposite way.'
'It does sometimes, evidently.'

3 'Blood and Fire' being a motto of the Salvation Army.
4 In Evangelical circles, including the Salvation Army, it was (and still is) often expected that an individual 'committing himself to God' will 'seal' the commitment by a public declaration or 'witness-bearing'.

'So it seems. But I've stayed over my time, so cheerio, and good luck!'

Two thoughtful men parted, Mac to continue the routine work of the unit, and the Padre to collect Lieutenant Woods and make their way up the line.

Chapter 9

Talking of Death and Censoring Letters

Looking inside a bivvy and noticing that Woods was by then ready to move off for his first visit to the gun positions, the Padre announced his readiness to start. Woods seemed a little hesitant and then addressed his partner, indicating a tin-hat, field-glasses, gas mask and other incidentals:

'I suppose we take all this paraphernalia up with us, Padre?'
'Yes, always those.'
'And revolvers?'
'Please yourself, but I don't think you will need one today. I hope not anyway!'

Then looking round, the Padre continued:

'You'll find field-glasses useful. It's the kind of day one may see some aerial activity.'

They were soon on their way and conversing freely as though a long friendship had existed between them. Common risks have the effect of dispensing with the usual preliminary cautions. Confidences are exchanged easily and are always respected.

'Is it a "hot soup" up there, Padre?'
'Not at all bad.'
'Any especial time of the day the scrapping usually takes place?'
'It's very quiet these days, you need fear nothing, this trip at least. A stray shell may come our way but you will soon get used to such things and not trouble. Instinct plays a large part out here and you will do well to trust it.'
'Yes! ... What sort of a fellow is the Battery Commander?'
'That all depends on you. He is splendid with a good man, but he has no time for one who does not make the honour of the Battery his first

concern. You'll find he will size you up pretty quickly, and usually he is very accurate. If you are a good soldier, you could not wish for a better chief.'

'Thanks!'

Nearing the gun-positions, they came to where a few shells were falling, but far enough away not to cause the Padre any concern – though his companion did seem to be not entirely at home. One came much nearer and there was a momentary pause, but conversation was soon resumed.

'What part of England are you from, Woods?'

'Plymouth, Padre.'

'My word, I'd like to be strolling along the Hoe this lovely morning.[1] I'm afraid we've got to do a bit of work before we shall have that privilege.'

'I reckon so. I suppose it has seemed a devil of a time to you out here. Do you think it will last much longer?'

'Things don't appear to be moving towards a conclusion. We are much as we were twelve months ago, as far as I can see. Something dramatic and sudden may wake us up soon.'

'I expect so.'

'In any case, old man, you will soon knuckle down to things. You can get used to anything, and while conditions may be rotten at times they do not kill us; they harden us, and we just jog along doing what we are told to do. That is how ... Look! There's a plane ... It's very low, too ... It's a Fritz!'

With lightning speed, the aeroplane swooped down and followed the direction of the open road along which the two men were walking. 'Get down!' shouted the Padre, and no sooner were the words uttered than there was the 'rat-tat-tat' of its machine-gun raking the road. With instinctive alertness the Padre fell in a heap in the ditch at the roadside, and dragged his pal in on top of him. A moment's hesitancy would have been fatal, for the bullets splashed the road within a few feet of their 'cover' and a couple of spent bullets fell alongside them. The whole incident took less than a minute and the plane had passed nearly out of sight when the men had recovered sufficiently to crawl out of the ditch. It had returned over the German lines before our surprised gunners, unused to these new hedge-hopping tactics, were able to train their guns on it.

---

1 Rider was brought up on the south coast of England.

'I say, Woods! That was a good christening for you, eh? Still that kind of thing does not happen often. You need not worry about every plane you see. We just happened to give him an easy target – so easy that he could not resist having a pot at us.'

'I hope not! It was a bit of a devil, wasn't it? Quite close enough for me.'

'Aye! And for me too. But it's all over now and it won't happen again today. Come along!'

And, a little shaken, both proceeded on their way.

Woods walked somewhat hesitantly, for he hardly knew what to expect next, and though that particular experience might not be repeated, there was the distinct possibility of something else equally disquieting. Normal conversation was soon resumed.

'Some men seem to be wonderfully fortunate even in war', said the Padre. 'There's always the chance that one may be the lucky fellow even in the worst situations and it is that that keeps us going. It's no good anticipating the worst, and though Tommy will have it that there are shells with men's names on them, you at least can be at ease, since no one knows you are here yet!'

'That's a thought.'

'Good fortune has been with me so far. It must be a dozen times at least that I have been missed by inches. The old Colonel calls me the mascot … I don't believe it's all luck, Woods. You'd expect me to say that, I suppose, but I do feel there are other factors that enter into things, even out here.'

'I don't know about that.'

'We haven't far to go now. Just through that village over there, or what's left of it – there's been some heavy scrapping there lately. It changed hands three times a week or two ago. It's certainly ours now and we intend to hold on to it. Our guns are two or three hundred yards in front of it. Here, this way, Woods.'

A little later, Woods suddenly and fearfully side-stepped to avoid something in his path, uttering an unintelligible half-smothered remark which attracted the attention of his companion. He had nearly trodden on the body of a dead German, whose blackened face and twisted shoulders were just visible from under the fallen rooftrees that had pinned him to the ground. Woods almost felt himself go pale, but he set his jaw and proceeded without further comment until, a little way along the road, he said:

'Do you know, Padre, that this is the first time I have seen death!'
'And not a good introduction to it either, Woods, but you will get used to it. It's a good thing we do get used to it, for life out here with too sensitive a nature would be absolutely intolerable. It's one of the rotten effects of war – one gets accustomed to degrading and cruel things. You'll have to fight hard, old man, to avoid losing the best things in your soul.'
'I am not sure that I have any to safeguard.'

Silently they continued their way and neared their destination.

Moving through a destroyed village still under enemy fire, where there was evidence of quite recent fighting in the form of dead victims of a bayonet charge, both officers silently raised their hats, caring little about Army customs concerning the wearing of headgear. At the far end of the village was a still intact archway through which they passed into a farmyard. Crossing this under cover of a boundary wall, they reached a well-worn pathway and continued along it in the welcome shelter of a small line of trees. So cleverly camouflaged in this setting that Woods had not noticed it was the first gun-pit of the Battery.

There were few signs of life, only one gunner doing guard duty. The Padre stopped at the top of a short flight of steps which led to a deep dugout, to announce his presence and that of Woods. The dim light of candles made recognition possible and the comradely greeting assured Woods that at least the gunnery officers were a friendly crowd.

'How are things, Sir?'
'It's fine up in the sunshine this glorious morning. May I introduce Woods to you? He has just joined us at the lines and Mac asked me to bring him along. Yesterday's Battery Order mentions his posting to us.'

Woods was left alone with his new chief. Conversation between them was soon established.

The Padre decided to stroll round the position and found the men taking their ease in neatly constructed bivvys which, by the aid of branches and sods, concealed their real significance.

'Good morning, lads. It's too bad having to spend such a day as this fighting wars, don't you think, lads?'
'It does and all, Sir! I'd rather be spendin' it with me gal at Brighton, I would an' all.'

'So would I – with my own, of course!'

'And I bet you would with mine too. See, 'ere she is, Sir.'

He handed over a dirty photograph with a good many stains from Flanders mud on it. From what one could see, the camera certainly had not flattered her even if it had done her justice, but to him she was the best to be had.

'I've gone a bit further than 'im, Sir. 'Ere's mine.'

A picture of a woman with three children was offered for inspection with the remark:

> 'And I won't be sorry neither when I can get back to 'em. Letters ain't much good to 'em. The bloomin' War Office won't let a fellow say nowt in them. How can a bloke say to his wife what 'e wants to say when 'e knows it's all gorn to be read by someone else what ain't married p'raps, and what don't understand like?'[2]
>
> 'It seems a bit hard, lads. But a war cannot be carried on without some sort of censorship. Even with all the precautions, Old Fritz seems to get hold of valuable information from somewhere. But you have nothing to fear from your officers censoring your letters; they are a jolly good lot. They don't like having to do it, and you can take it from me they never discuss what any of you say. They are as human as you are when it comes to letter writing, and you can trust them with your secrets, if what you have to say is worth saying. It may do them good to know what you think of all your folk at home. I'll tell you what I'll do. If I can count on your loyalty to me, I'll put you on your honour in this matter. You write all you want to say to your wives and sweethearts in your letters and then pass them on to me, unsealed, and I'll not read them but send them on for you. Just one here and there I shall have to select to safeguard myself, though I don't reckon fellows like you, after you have given me your word, would let me down.'

'No d... fear, Sir! That's sportin'. Thank you!'

Almost every journey he made after that, the Padre was called upon to act as confidential postman. Only on one occasion did the letter selected for censorship give rise to any difficulty, and then it was because the privilege

---

2 The anecdote most likely relates to 1917, when Rider himself was 'someone what ain't married'.

was being abused to serve a purpose for which it was not intended. The letter was a tirade against a wife who evidently had given cause for some complaint. The lines became more and more vitriolic, and however disinterested one might be in the actual quarrel, to allow such a letter to pass would offend the Padre's sense of fitness. It was handed back to the sender with the suggestion that, if it were modified somewhat, it would be more likely to do good than if forwarded in its present form. It was replaced by another which suggested that the heat was lessening – although the temperature had gone down only a little.

Normal letter censoring was a part of the Padre's education. After wading through a hundred of them, he wondered why the English language should require a Standard Dictionary running into eight volumes to convey men's thoughts to others. When there did not appear to be an appropriate word already in use, Tommy was a master at coining one. Remarkably few words serve for all purposes, for pathos, pity or piety. At times, he felt tempted to make a few minor corrections to assist the reader rather than the writer, as in the following case. 'I see Bessie's had her young man killed.' Foul play not suspected! A little re-arrangement of the words would have served a good purpose also in this letter. 'I had a b... bullet in me back the other day and if me entrenching tool hadn't been there too well I would not have been telling you it.' It was not the grammar but the confidence that contributed to the censor's education.

Chapter 10

Gas and Bombs

The strong healing rays of the sun blessed a beautiful morning and roused from their sleep the men of the battery. As soon as they took their stations at the guns, they noticed aloft in the skies a row of five 'Sausages', British observation balloons, a backcloth to the activities at the guns.[1] But almost immediately, as an introduction to the day's happenings, dropping vertically out of the skies, or so it seemed, an enemy plane swooped down and emptied its ammunition belt of incendiary bullets into the envelope of Number One Balloon. In a few seconds this began to fall in flames. The observers aboard, jumping away from the fireball, had not had time to open their parachutes and so fell headlong just in advance of the blazing mass. Then the plane, sweeping along the line like an arrow from a bow, meted out similar treatment to the remaining four balloons. So well done and quickly executed had the movement been that all five falling craft were in descent at the same time, several of them carrying their human freight with them. But a few minutes later, four or five parachutes could be seen slowly bearing human forms to the ground, this giving a measure of relief to the surprised ground staff who had been so completely outwitted.

That morning, enemy planes were directing artillery fire at our guns with almost uncanny accuracy. But the shells struck the ground with feeble explosions. Such ineffective stuff was it that the gunners joked about Jerry's 'second-hand puff-balls', and seemed not to attach much importance to the bombardment. When in the ranks the Padre had had his baptism of fire of all kinds, and had learned the wisdom of being always on the safe side in cases of doubt. He had a strong suspicion that these were gas shells, although gas had until then always been sent over

---

1 Later it is noted that the Germans are also flying observation balloons.

in cylinders, and he began to detect a familiar smell. Instinctively he gave the alarm of 'GAS!', at the same time plunging his face into his gas mask.[2]

The men were inclined to scorn the warning, crediting the Padre with 'getting the wind-up', but in a few minutes they learned that something unusual had indeed happened and that they were the victims of new devices. Their throats began to dry up and to swell, and their eyes filled with tears.[3] Fright also added its unnerving element, and soon there was commotion. The stretcher-bearers and the Padre were kept busy for a considerable time. Only one officer at the battery had escaped, and he was the youngest member of the staff, the man who a few days before had made his first trip to the 'line' in the company of the Padre, now again his only companion. Woods, being a fresher, was still indisposed to take risks, and owed his escape from the gas to questioning the sincerity of a warning after he had heeded it, and not before.

The C.O. had always affirmed that gas casualties were due to carelessness, hence none of the officer casualties was willing to go down to the dressing-station to report himself a victim.[4] Woods carried on the duties of battery officer while his three brother officers were lying hors-de-combat on the ground in their dugout.

'What do you think I ought to do, Padre?' asked Woods.

'Well, it certainly is a rotten position in which to find yourself. I

---

2 Gas as a form of attack was first used on the Western Front, by the Germans, in April 1915 (it had earlier been used on the Eastern Front), and was used by both sides thereafter. It was at first, and then throughout the war, released from cylinders, but this required a constant wind in the right direction, even when the cylinders were lobbed towards the enemy. After several disasters to the releasing side, gas shells were developed, and by 1916 both sides had them. Although deadlier gases than the original tear-gas (xylyl bromide) came into use, for instance chlorine by 1917, gas remained more of a threat than an effective weapon, its nuisance value lying in the necessity of carrying gas masks and wearing them, making other action difficult at moments of alarm. Rider's infantry experience of gas was, in fact, probably very limited. When on the Arras front, in May 1916, the battalion had a 'gas alert', and in June a British raid preceded by a gas cloud was observed (Fairclough, pp. 50, 52), while the shelling before the German raid on the neighbouring battalion on 4 June included gas shells (Carter, p. 157). During the Somme battles of July the British were prepared to use gas (*Military Operations, Appendices*, e.g., p. 160), but do not seem to have done so, and there appear to have been no gas attacks on the battalion. Although Rider may have undergone a training exercise in which soldiers were exposed to whiffs of gas, this episode may have been his first experience of being involved in a successful gas attack.

3 This description, and the fact that all the sufferers appear to have recovered without serious consequences, indicates that the gas was tear-gas. Rider later refers to casualties severely, perhaps fatally, affected by gas, in this case probably chlorine or phosgene (Chapter 14).

4 By 1917 the latest gas masks were considered to afford total protection against the gases so far used.

should hang on a bit longer, for I think this is no more than the old tear-gas, and so not very lasting.'

'I feel I daren't report to the C.O. He'll curse like blazes.'

'He will that, but it cannot alter the situation. Look here, you cannot leave the guns. You carry on here and I'll go back and tell him what has happened.'

'That's a d... good suggestion, Padre, I shall be profoundly thankful if you'll do that.'

A glance at the officer casualties and an attempt at conversation with them revealed that the situation was not improving, and so, with a parting 'best of luck to you', the Padre set out on his unpleasant errand.

Woods found the other battery on his flank similarly unstaffed, but as the shelling had ceased and all was quiet there was little ground for anxiety about the gun-position itself, and he was able to give most of his time to trying to rouse his messmates. A whole hour passed before any signs of recovery were seen. The first one to respond was the senior officer. Replying to an enquiry about what had happened, Woods related how badly the whole Brigade had suffered and what he had done in the matter of reporting events to the Brigade Commander.

'Why did you not consult me first?'

'I tried too often, Sir, but you were unable to advise me.'

'It's deuced hard luck, and there will be the devil to pay over this.'

'I am sorry, Sir, but it seemed the only thing for me to do.'

'I suppose it was. Is everybody else O.K. now?'

'I'm afraid not. You are the only one besides myself who knows much about anything yet. Look down here!'

He pointed along the dugout to where the other two officers of the mess were still prostrate. 'Oh hell!' the other remarked as he made the effort to see them and then sank down again to try to think what to do.

'They'll recover shortly, as you have done, Sir. Lie still a bit. There is no urgency, I'll go out on the position and see how they are getting on there.'

Woods was able to report favourably and many of the men were already on the move again.

Away at Headquarters, the Brigade Commander was sitting smoking his pipe and wading through the 'Orders' received from a still higher authority, when the familiar form of the Padre entered.

'Good afternoon, Sir!'

'Hullo, Padre! Is everything O.K.?'

'I'm afraid not, Sir. The positions have been badly drenched with gas shells this morning and some of our fellows, little suspecting the nature of the bombardment, have been overcome. It was not until the mischief had been done that they realised the situation.'

'What do you mean – mischief? Are there many concerned?'

'Quite a number, Sir, knocked out at least for a time. Woods was the only officer left at the battery to carry on when I left, but the others were coming round. I don't think it is very bad, Sir, but you know how gas scares men when they are not used to it. He is carrying on until they have pulled themselves together. But he thought it was his duty to let you know, Sir.'

'I should think so. The ... fools. Do they think Old Fritz is going to tie labels on his bally shells? It's ... carelessness: my Brigade too – letting me down like a lot of ... I'll ...'

'Sir! It would have been a good man not to have been caught, for it was a very clever and quick bit of work, involving the whole brigade front simultaneously. None of the officers would entertain the idea of leaving the guns, and by now, I expect, they are at their job again. Woods asked me to call in and tell you, but he did not think it needed a written report.'

'He didn't think so, eh! How the devil is it that the most inexperienced of the lot of them should be the one to miss it? You of course would: it's your usual luck.'

'He's already learnt the wisdom of "Safety First" when there is any uncertainty, Sir.'

'Some rotten thing like this is bound to happen just when it's least wanted. We are short-handed enough, God knows, without throwing ourselves away like this. There's no one down here I can send up. Only one officer is left at the waggon lines in each battery. We never know what might be wanted these days.'

'Could I be of any service to you, Sir?'

'What the devil do you know about artillery? It would be ... the silly fools ...'

Gradually the infuriated Commander calmed down, giving the Padre another opportunity to speak.

'Surely, Sir, one need not be a trained gunner to be able to do something useful at a time like this. I won't let you down if you will entrust some little service to me.'

'Sorry, Padre, but you know how a daft show like this lets me down. Forgive me for "letting rip"; you'd d... well would too; I ...'

'Well, Sir, what shall it be?'

'I'm dashed if I know what you or anyone else can do. Ah! There's one thing that has to be done at once. An ammo column of six limbers has to go up there before night, and Potts is the only one down here who knows the exact position of the guns and he can ill be spared now – it would leave no one here.'

'Well, Sir, that is a job I can do. I know the way, every inch of it; and if the Sergeant-Major is there to give the commands, I'll see the column arrives at its destination. Give me the opportunity, Sir!'

'Good! That will help things a bit. Thank you! Tell them I'll be up myself soon.'

'Leave it to me, Sir, and I'll deliver the goods.'

The Colonel addressed his groom. 'Bombardier! See that the Padre has a good mount. Give him my number two if necessary.' 'Yes, Sir!' Feeling a bit self-conscious, the Padre, safely mounted on the allotted charger, rode up to the Sergeant-Major who had already got the column lined up on the road, and taking up his position in front, gave him the order to advance. It was already getting dusk, and the journey, about one and a half miles, lay through country strange to all but the Padre, for the present gun-position had been taken up only two days before. Proceeding across a field, then through a coppice and a little way along a road, a halt was called under the shelter of a hedge that marked the side of a farmyard. More than once on the journey the Gunners hinted that the column was lost, and 'It's a long way to Tipperary' was softly sung with appropriate new words. But they were wrong.

The supply delivered, the Sergeant-Major, eager to get back home, addressed Woods: 'Everything's O.K., Sir! I know the way back. Shall I carry on?' And almost without waiting for permission, he took his place at the head of the column and gave the order to march. When sufficient distance separated him from the consenting officer this developed into a trot, and the waggons and horses were soon lost in the darkness. The Padre expressed his usual good wishes and took his own departure. He had gone only about half a mile when he met the Brigade Commander on his way up to see things for himself.

'How goes it now, Padre?'

'Almost normal again, Sir!'

'I shall not be here long, so we can go back together. Wait for me. We shall all be home in time for a good night's rest.'

Having cooled down after his first reactions to the news, and having sampled a little of the front-line feeling, the Brigade Commander launched a considerably modified *strafe* on the half-frightened staff at the guns. Being reassured that everything would proceed according to instructions, he rejoined the Padre, and talking about other things the two officers made their way to a night's rest. It was too late when the Padre arrived at the waggon lines for him to think of returning that night to his place at the guns, and he was glad to accept the invitation to 'kip down' with Potts in a small shack near the horse lines.[5] 'I have to go up to relieve Woods at midnight, Padre, and you can have my bed over there in the corner.' This was an offer the Padre was so willing to accept that in less than ten minutes he was sound asleep. He remembered nothing more until just after one o'clock, when the arrival of Woods disturbed him. Neither man seemed much interested just then in his companion, so dead tired were they both, and in another ten minutes they joined each other in rendering their respective parts in a wonderful snoring duet; one which seemed to be a deliberate concerted item for expressing gratitude.

About two a.m., however, both men became subconsciously aware of the droning of aeroplanes. They were roused to full consciousness almost immediately by a shout from the guard – 'Lights out!' The whole complement of men at the 'lines' automatically responded, and everyone became wide-awake, knowing all too well the significance of such a command. The increasing noise indicated the approach in their direction of whatever it was in the air, and there was little time for speculation. The unmistakable swishing sound that accompanies falling bombs made it patent that a whole cargo of them had been released from a plane passing immediately overhead. With remarkable accuracy of aim, the deadly things landed right among the tethered horses, where they exploded with terrific force. From the enemy's point of view, it had been a bit of splendid work, the success of which was due largely to the good work of the observers in the balloons which had been up over the enemy positions all the previous morning. The horses had been placed as near as possible to one another, in a square, in order to offer the smallest target in any emer-

---

5 Seemingly the Padre slept at the gun site, probably in a dugout.

gency, but direct hits having been registered, the results were disastrous. The whole place had been transformed into a shambles of bleeding and lacerated animals, who bore their pain in their pathetic silence.

When the drone of the planes indicated that they were speeding home, the men were called to their stations by Woods. Through good fortune every man was able to answer at the roll call, but to reach their 'muster stations' nearly all had to stumble over broken ropes, fallen animals, yards from where they had been tied, and also had to avoid the terror-stricken animals that were loose. Woods and the Padre followed the men round with electric torches, trying to estimate the damage. Returning to his bivvy, Woods secured his revolver and a generous supply of cartridges, and resumed his investigation of the casualties. For an hour and a half the two officers were busy feeling with their hands the bloody bodies of the horses, till either their fingers or their whole hands located the wounds. Where these were slight they were dressed with wads and iodine; where they were ugly and extensive, a carefully aimed bullet near the 'blaze' put the creature out of its agony. ' 'Ere, Sir, this one quick!', and ' 'Ere, Sir, too!', came as frequent requests from sympathetic drivers when they saw the plight of their charges.

When duty was completed that evening there was little of the night left, so the men sat together in their dugout till the coming of dawn gave them the opportunity for further investigation of the damage done. The rays of the sun failed to relieve the scene of its desolation. The complement of horses had been reduced by twenty-three and many others were detailed for a journey, if at all possible, to the Veterinary Surgeon's Depôt. Fortunately the men's injuries were confined to those mental ones caused by separation from their old pals. Some of the men were really bereaved and had not recovered from their grief when the Padre strolled round the broken lines after an early breakfast.

'Sir!', said one man, 'I've bin wi' them two 'osses for nigh on three years now and them was real chums. I'm sorry them's gone, Sir!'

'So am I, Driver. It was a bad night for all of us, eh?'

'Yes, Sir! Yer see, I'd got to lovin' them. I ain't got no one else in the world that's anything to me. Father and Mother's gone long ago, and it didn't make much difference to me, for they didn't bother 'bout me, nor me them. Our 'ome 'adn't no love in it, and I've 'ad more of that from Jess and Old Bob than from all of them put together.'

'I'm sorry, Driver, that you had to wait for a pair of horses to learn what love can mean to a man. It won't always be like that for you, I hope. He who made love for us has something even greater than you have learned so far, my man!'

'One never knows, does one, Sir?'

And the driver turned to washing blood from the leg of one poor battered beast trying to hobble along to the horses' hospital.

Comradeship and cannibalism seem quite compatible with one another. The condition of war bridged the centuries back to the days when our forefathers were less sentimental. A savoury meal goes a long way to heal a broken heart. 'I'm sure Old Bob will be pleased when he knows how much I'm enjoying this bit out of his rump! Bless 'im!'[6]

---

6 Eating a favourite horse is repeated in Chapter 15.

Chapter 11

A Bad Job

In one part of the line the trench system had become very elaborate. During the long spell in which no movement in either direction had taken place, full advantage was taken of the dry and hard condition of the ground to make the defences safe and comfortable. This had been so well done that that district was known as 'cushy'. Carefully screened outlets and inlets to the trenches, and unusually good accommodation in dugouts for the troops, made men feel both safe and fortunate. Such were the conditions in what were known as the defences of the town of Arras, situated near the northern end of the British Front.

Beneath the town itself, excavation work had been carried out in the past, in order to secure good building stone, a commodity also much in demand in the more recent days. As a consequence of the excavations, a host of caverns, large and small, existed within the very foundations of the houses, or in some cases provided extensive cellar accommodation for the less important stores of business premises. These places had been called into service for more important work. During the siege of the town and through many troublous periods, some civilians had chosen to stay there rather than chance their fate on the roads as refugees, and by sheer necessity others had been compelled to remain. Nearly five hundred of the normal population were still in the town. Added to this number were crowds of people from outside the town who had been forced to abandon their homes when these had fallen within the fighting zone, or too close to it. All these individuals had found the caves good sanctuaries, since they were practically invulnerable to any kind of long-distance bombardment. Many older and many more timid folk had lived underground for long periods, coming out into the open only when they needed fresh air or food supplies.

The town was garrisoned by troops living in the least damaged residences. Between them and their cellar companions a friendship sprang up which gave the civilians a feeling of security. Having recently suffered from shelling and bombing, the town had very few places that remained undamaged. Many streets were blocked by fallen houses. The *Petite Place* looked sad and forsaken, its fine square of Spanish houses, built by the prisoners of a much earlier war, showing big gaping wounds. The once fine *Hôtel-de-Ville*, with its tall spire – a particularly splendid bit of Flemish architecture, but one that the enemy had used as an aiming-guide – had been reduced to a heap of smashed masonry.

Outside the town, conditions were bad. Villages which had given shelter to thousands of the displaced townspeople had become terribly overcrowded. People of varied temperaments, some penniless, had had to share houses. How could relationships be other than strained when sometimes two or more refugee families competed for rights or privileges in quarters belonging to no one in particular, the previous owners or tenants having fled? Often far less bad blood existed between the two enemy forces than between fellow citizens called upon to share a common distress.

A small-scale attack had pushed the front line from its original place in the suburbs to about a mile into the country. This put the troglodyte population out of range of the smaller artillery that had for so long harassed them. Some people, eager to grasp any opportunity to regain possession of their old homes in the suburbs, decided to face the risks involved. But disappointment was often their only reward, for they found their houses wrecked or commandeered by the military. Moreover, when they returned to their old quarters these had been taken over by new squatter tenants, with the result that they were compelled to travel further away, behind the lines, to seek sanctuary.

In the town itself, a few souls were eking out an existence by making souvenirs to sell to the troops, using material rescued from the ruined cathedral, the *Hôtel-de-Ville* or other places of interest. Some individuals had opened cafés in parts of houses not entirely demolished, where soldiers and civilians congregated in their spare moments for refreshment and conversation. Others again attempted to carry on, in skeleton form, the business and shopping life of the place. Sometimes when the renewed activities of the town were at their height a salvo of long-range shells would fall and send most of those on the streets scurrying back to their cellars. Above ground would then be left to a few siege-hardened individuals who had lost all fear and found something exhilarating in courting disaster.

REFLECTIONS ON THE BATTLEFIELD

The months and days dragged on. Then, one day, troops in large numbers were seen to be on the move, many detailed for billets within the town but many others passing right through it. Whole brigades, one of South African troops, were crowded into the remaining empty places below ground, with strict orders to conceal themselves as much as possible, so as not to arouse the suspicions of the civilians or reward the keen eyes of the observers on enemy planes.[1] Some civilians welcomed these signs of imminent activity, associating it with possible deliverance, but others resented them lest a failure should make things infinitely worse. Probably the general wish was to 'let sleeping dogs lie', but this was not the intention of the military authority, and secret orders in the hands of local headquarters indicated serious business ahead. During the night, the troops which had been in the cellars were moved forward, their places being taken by still more troops entering the town. The following day, Easter Sunday – a day which caused those with a Christian background to reflect on the significance of forthcoming events in a state of peace of mind – troops and guns were concentrated on the outskirts of the town for an offensive to be launched at dawn the next morning.[2]

The commanders of the attacking troops knew the magnitude of the task set them, the enemy positions being particularly strong. For two years the Germans had occupied a splendid position on a ridge overlooking the town, and between their trenches and those of the British was a veritable forest of barbed-wire entanglements. As a second line of defence, the enemy had exploited the advantage offered by a long, high railway embankment, which was flanked on each side by an equally useful

---

1 A South African division participated in the battles on the Somme in mid-1916, and a memorial to South African dead stands at Delville (Cruttwell, p. 270). But South Africans also served later. Perhaps Rider mentions them here because of a later reference to a South African, in Chapter 14.
2 Rider describes the 'Battle of Arras' which began, as he says, on Easter Monday, 9 April 1917, and which had some limited territorial success, particularly in the capture of Vimy Ridge which had threatened the British line. 'The town of Arras had been made a vast underground repository for reserves. Its cellars had been interconnected and lit with electricity. The troops emerged from them into the communication trenches ... The fresh divisions were readily available to pass through the original attacking troops and to continue the advance without interruption by the manoeuvre known as "leap-frogging" ... the creeping barrage and aeroplane liaison worked admirably ... Arras is the last battle in which mounted troops were used in a crater-field ... a whole corps had been brought into Arras on the night of the 8th ... [but] the concentration of cavalry ... actually impeded the infantry ...' (Cruttwell, pp. 405–8). The artillery barrage preparatory to the infantry attack employed a larger proportion of high-velocity shells than earlier in the war, these shells being more capable of penetrating and destroying enemy fortifications.

'cutting'. Much time and labour had fortified this sector to make it almost impregnable. Its extensive and deep dugouts, accommodating large numbers of enemy troops, were protected with ferro-concrete emplacements serving as look-out and gun positions.

It was, therefore, with feelings of serious responsibility, but also of resolution, that the attackers prepared to strike. They had to work to a carefully prepared programme, the opening of the attack being signalled by fierce and concentrated artillery bombardment in the form of a 'barrage'. Salvoes of shells of every description tore great gaps in the entanglements, to form passages through. Then, as if by a magic touch, the range of the guns lengthened to drop their fire on to the enemy first-line trenches. While the occupants were crouching for shelter from the terrible destruction, the British troops scaled the parapets of their trenches and strolled over 'no-man's-land', with superb calmness, until they reached a point close to the enemy positions, from which they were screened by the smoke and flame of the bursting shells. Again, at a given signal, the range lengthened till the shells were dropped well behind the enemy front line, making the task of reinforcing it a matter of extreme danger. At that moment, without allowing the enemy sufficient time to collect himself, the storming troops threw themselves upon his position and carried it with but little opposition. In a rapid advance, line after line fell into the hands of the British, who took prisoners in substantial numbers. At the same time, in the town, the opening of the bombardment had been the signal for the advance of the reserve troops sheltering there and they poured out from their cellars.

The roads leading to the town, which had been deserted for months, soon became almost choked with the traffic of guns moving up into new positions, ammunition convoys with extra munitions for the hungry guns, and reserve battalions coming forward to support the advance. The unusual sight of a regiment of cavalry preparing for action so enheartened the Tommies that they greeted it with cheers, since this suggested a form of battle very different from the trench warfare they had known for so many long months. Despite the congestion on the roads, a passage was opened up for the many stretcher cases being carried down. Remarks were exchanged between the men on the stretchers and their comrades going up the line, some men congratulating themselves on their good fortune in getting a 'Blighty one'.[3] But a new spirit seemed to animate everyone, and

---

3 A 'Blighty wound' was one which was minor and only sufficiently serious to require the soldier to be sent to recover in a hospital in Britain ('Blighty'), with the possibility of some sick leave at home.

the coming of a new hope about the outcome of the war had made the 'broken' and the 'whole' equally heroic and eager.

The Padre had taken up his post in an Advanced Dressing-Station that had been established in a long dugout in a sunken road about a mile behind the original front line. Soon after 'zero hour' he made his way along the road in the direction of the advance, and was hailed by an infantry Commanding Officer whose battalion was halted at the roadside awaiting orders to move forward.

'This is a great show Padre, eh? But I've had a bit of bad luck already.'

'I'm sorry to hear that, Sir. What is it?'

'A shell has just robbed me of three of my best young officers. They were conferring with one another just along the road there. We've laid them at the side of the bank there, just by the factory gate. Do you think you could give them a decent burial? They are worth one; they've been good fellows.'

'I will, Sir. Could you spare a few men with shovels now? And we may be able to do it right away, while we're halted. We may never get the chance later. I'm at your service now.'

Six men were detailed to dig a grave, a common one, in a secluded spot within the factory yard, and not many yards from where the fateful shell had done its deadly work less than half an hour before. The task was completed and, at the invitation of the Padre, the Commanding Officer, with most of his fellow officers, and a few men from the depleted platoons, gathered round to pay their tribute of respect to their fallen comrades. A very reverent Committal Service was conducted and the incident closed with the Colonel's remark: 'They were worthy of the best the Church could do for them, in the hour of their premature dismissal from service.' In a few minutes the grave was filled in, and the order to march was given. The Battalion moved to its destined place in the line, and the Padre to anywhere where he felt his services might be called upon. In the space of a few hours, a score of similar demands were made upon him.

Later in the day, he met the same C.O., who came in time to help him lift to the roadside another poor fellow. He had died in the arms of the Padre, as he attempted to carry him from his dangerous position in the middle of the road, where a few minutes before a stray shell had found another victim. Carefully and reverently, two officers took the body from the Padre and laid it at the roadside. The C.O. remarked as they separated:

'Goodbye, Padre! Mine's a pretty bad job at times, but I'm d... glad I haven't yours. The best of luck to you!'

The Padre greatly appreciated the officer's benediction on his day's work.

Chapter 12

Prisoners not Enemies

Running parallel with the trenches in one particular sector was a canal that once bore its fleet of barges transporting their cargoes of flax to the mills which at intervals graced the banks.[1] In those happier days, delightful little lanes led to the canal and crossed it by means of ornamental bridges, well balanced and easily operated by hand, and it was the delight of the little children of the bargees to run ahead of their craft and operate the levers to let their father's 'ship' pass. All this had changed. The water was low and dirty, in places covered with the green scum that denoted stagnation. Artillery fire had put the bridges out of action, leaving them as twisted iron-work and derelict. Trestled wooden bridges had replaced them, revealing the resourcefulness of the Royal Engineers. The motionless stagnant water was occasionally disturbed by an exploding shell which churned up the mud at the bottom, causing an offensive smell as the decomposed body of a soldier or a horse would make its protest at being disturbed from its resting place. The bank, no longer the towpath of peace-loving bargees, was a dirty, shell-marked way trodden by hundreds of soldiers making their journeys to and from the trenches. In front of the canal was desolate flat country dividing the 'supports' from the semi-trenched, sandbagged positions that represented the front line. The whole area was generously pitted with shell holes of every description and size, and these were hidden from view through being waterlogged. Villages and roads alike had been blown out of existence by months of artillery fire and the only route possible to the forward area was along narrow trench-board tracks for troops, and on hurriedly constructed roads consisting of tree trunks laid side by side, for transport.

1 Canals were close to several stretches of the British front, but this is presumably the Yser Canal near Ypres, since the next chapter dates the present episode to the 'Battle of Ypres', that is, the Third Battle of Ypres, known as Passchendaele, begun in July 1917.

Where the canal banks rose above the level of the surrounding land they lent themselves to defence works and many tunnels honeycombed the sides farthest from the enemy, providing both billeting quarters for troops and storehouses for equipment of all kinds. One more ambitious attempt at excavation was formed into an Advanced Dressing-Station. Across the eighteen hundred yards of desolation in front, traffic was restricted to that which could be carried on after dark, and it was the easiest possible thing for one to lose one's way. Even in daylight everything had been made to look alike, just parts of a devastated country without landmarks of any kind. Men making their way along the duckboard track during the night would often find that it ended suddenly, yet not at the point that had originally marked its limit. An explosion sometimes carried away a whole section of it. Then the men would have to feel round in the dark to try to discover fresh boards that marked the continuation of the track, but often they struck only a single, isolated one which had been deposited where it was after a flight through the air in an entirely different direction. Occasionally, after a considerable journey along the newly discovered way, a man found himself back where he had begun his trip.

At one point there were the remnants of a small Decaville railway system which, when the front line was much further away, had been a busy line for light enemy transport.[2] By now the track was broken and out of action, its small motor-tractor lying abandoned near two small trucks on their sides, these adding to the scene of general disorder. It was in this area that the Padre found himself on the eve of a battle, sharing quarters with the Medical Officer, whose surgery was in the cellar of the ruined farmhouse alongside of which the railway ran.

The attack had been a great success, but casualties were heavy and the services of the Aid Post staff were in great demand. To add to the difficulties, an armed guard of two men had brought in a batch of seventeen German prisoners and had been instructed to leave them at the Aid Post, so that they might be used as stretcher-bearers.[3] Many walking-wounded had already arrived, and others were coming in assisting more serious cases, some of whom, through exhaustion, had to become stretcher cases

---

2 The Decauville (not Decaville) system was a form of railed tramway, easily laid over flat ground, and used during the war to transport supplies up to and near the front. For photographs of a railed tramway, perhaps of this system, used for carrying casualties to a dressing-station, see Carter, pp. 169, 184.

3 For photographs of German prisoners acting as stretcher-bearers, see Carter, pp. 216, 225. Chaplain Bickersteth once found himself in charge of 200 Germans acting as stretcher-bearers for 'our wounded', and 'they worked very well' (*Bickersteth* JB, p. 170).

as soon as they arrived. To relieve the Medical Officer, the Padre had made himself responsible for the evacuation of the wounded, since there was grave congestion at a point very vulnerable to both shellfire and aeroplane attack. In the midst of the proceedings, a low-flying enemy plane was seen to be approaching and this drove those capable of movement to seek cover anywhere it could be found.

The number of wounded was so great that soon all the ordinary methods of evacuation were taxed to the limit, and an ever-increasing number was assembled at the post. The idle railway was a challenge to the Padre, and he decided to make an inspection of the stock to ascertain whether it could by any means be pressed into service. The investigation resulted in a length of about a mile being commissioned for duty, and with the aid of a few German prisoners the scattered remnants of the system were collected together and the line opened. But the engine was not a ready starter, and it was not until a few repairs, mostly with wire from what had been barbed-wire defences, had been effected that it became operational. With its engine 'active' and the engineer at his post, the spitting loco made its protest against being called upon to re-enter service, yet did agree under pressure to pull its load. During the many short spurts of movement, the train seemed to enjoy a special dispensation of luck. Its escapes from destruction were many. Time and time again only a few feet saved it from a direct hit; once it was machine-gunned from the air; another time it was derailed by subsidence.

The German prisoners at the post seemed eager to assist, and though they were not officially eligible for more than one journey, they volunteered for other journeys, knowing that many of their own fellows were among the casualties to be removed. Five loads, each of four walking cases and two stretcher cases, were conveyed down the line to within easy reach of the dressing-station on the canal bank. The sun was sinking and the prisoners of war were supposed to be put into their 'cage' before sundown. But where exactly either the military police or their prisoners' cages were, no one at the post had the slightest idea. How the men were to be taken there was also a problem, since there were no armed men available to act as escort. A tired M.O.,[4] his exhausted stretcher-bearers, and the Padre were the only British within sight. It therefore fell to the Padre to escort the prisoners.

Mounting the locomotive, the Padre called to the Germans to 'jump in', and he hoped to run the entire contingent back to the canal bank. Soon

4 Medical Officer

all were aboard, but most had to get out again to give the locomotive a push to get it going. It refused, there being not a single attempt on the part of the plugs to spark. All save the driver had dismounted and it was hoped that a longer and faster push might do the trick, but this failed too. The unwilling machine decided the fate of the men. They had to walk. Seventeen disgruntled, tired and hungry prisoners stood in the fast-falling darkness awaiting orders. But there was no one to give them.

Delay was dangerous as it was almost dark. Long since the prisoners should have been handed over to the custody of the police and should have been under a strong guard. There was no alternative for the Padre and he realised he would have to accept responsibility for them for at least a little while longer. Motioning to them to 'fall in' behind him, he set out 'in faith', with the meagre information that there was a prisoners' cage somewhere on the other side of the canal, but at least a mile away. Slowly the 'file' set out along the duckboard track, which was slippery and very uneven. The deepening darkness made it impossible for the leader to keep his eye on the whole line and he had a feeling of insecurity through being completely unarmed. He therefore decided it was a wiser and safer policy to take his place at the back of the line, and to trust to the leading prisoner to grope his own way along the boards.

As long as this track remained intact all was well. But after a short distance there was a halt, and enquiry revealed that the track had ended in a break. However, the other side of the break was soon traced, and the whole party was again making good progress when an unfortunate incident called for resourcefulness. One member of the party collapsed under the heavy strain of a long day and fell into the mud at the side of the track. In the darkness, by then growing intense, it was extremely difficult to deal with him as the duckboards were the only possible place where he could be laid. These were muddy and greasy and almost indistinguishable from the mud around; furthermore, they were so narrow that those who rendered first aid had to stand in the inches-deep mud at the sides. The only restorative at hand consisted of the few remaining dregs from the water bottles of the entire party. These, when pooled, amounted to very little, since during the day the thirsty men had sucked their bottles almost dry. Twenty minutes passed before the man was sufficiently recovered to resume the journey, but good progress was then made for a further half mile. At that point, the track suddenly ended at a huge hole, where boards were lying in confusion everywhere. In the almost total darkness, the task of trying to trace the next stretch of consecutive boards was undertaken by the first few men in the file, the remainder of the party halting where they were. The Padre had stepped to the front to ascertain the position, and in about five minutes, he being satisfied that all was well, the party resumed the tramp. This time the Padre led the column and the prisoners had to keep in touch with him as best they could.

Then came the familiar and unmistakable sound of the approach, through the air high above, of a large shell. The whole party instinctively ducked for protection, and the explosion of the shell when it plunged into the nearby slush splashed them from head to foot with mud. The sudden concerted action of the men put an undue strain on a duckboard that was supporting two of them, and it went slithering into the mud at the bottom of a deep shell hole, carrying them with it. This taxed human endurance a little too severely and there followed much angry conversation amongst the men, continuing for several moments, and it was obvious that they were feeling rebellious. Not understanding the language, the Padre was unable to issue any command that suited the occasion, and he felt at a loss to know quite how to act. He did not know whether they were contemplating escape, revolt or something even worse, seeing that he was absolutely at their mercy. It was an ugly situation and in his helplessness he breathed a silent appeal to God for guidance. In response, as so often happens, an unprecedented reaction solved the emergency. He attempted to regain control by recourse to the use of stern, staccato English, uttered in a tone at least an octave lower than was usual with him, in the hope that it would sound impressive and authoritative. Simultaneously, as if by instinct, he made a quick movement with his right hand to the hip pocket of his breeches and grasped the flap tightly. This action was interpreted by those in the immediate vicinity, as it was intended to be, as one of arming himself with a loaded revolver, and this had the effect of restoring order and quiet.[5]

By this time he had the further unpleasant feeling that he had lost his way. Whatever happened, he felt he must keep that fact from the men as long as possible. It was not to be for long, however, for they had sensed the situation by almost immediate telepathy, and they began exchanging hasty words with one another. Though the Padre was unable to under-

---

5 Chaplain Bickersteth was supervising a group of German prisoners transporting stretchers carrying wounded when one of them 'let the stretcher fall at his end', tipping out the occupant. Bickersteth, enraged, struck the prisoner with his stick and, to frighten him further, borrowed a revolver from an officer and 'made some significant signs with it towards the young German' (*Bickersteth* JB, p. 272).

stand their remarks, he felt sure that they were directed at him and his leadership. His answer to this challenge was to continue in the direction he had been taking with a brisk step that suggested confidence. Again the unexpected happened. His heart leaped for joy when a voice speaking English reached his ear, out of the darkness and from a position very close at hand. He paused to allow an approaching individual to pass, but nothing happened for a few seconds, and no one appeared. The silence was broken by his challenge – 'Who's there?' It was answered, in English, by one of the prisoners who stepped out of the line and drew alongside – and then offered his services as interpreter! The conversation that followed provided a cheering interlude. The Padre learned that before the war the German prisoner had been in a large business house in the heart of London, and there had gained a good knowledge of the English language. The fact that he held the rank of Corporal was an added advantage, for it placed him as a kind of 'buffer' between the Padre and the less orderly members of the party. So in their common distress, a friendship sprang up which was as sincere as that between any two brothers-in-arms, though in this instance friend and foe covenanted with one another.

Over two hours had been occupied on the journey so far, and it was the assurance, given in English to the Corporal and passed on in German, that it was nearing completion that rallied the party to resume the tramp at a quicker pace. Five minutes more passed, and then with a feeling of profound thankfulness the Padre noticed, looming up a few yards in front, what he thought must be the raised bank of the canal. This being confirmed, his gratitude was so sincere that instinctively he breathed a prayer that must have been audible. An opening in the bank was found that led to the canal itself, which was crossed at that point by a rickety bridge, latterly abandoned for a stronger one erected some distance farther along. The party trusted itself, in single file, over this precarious support, and completed the crossing without mishap. Soon the path leading from it opened out on to a roadway that led unmistakably back towards the British base. Its solid foundation, contrasted with the slippery duckboard track, put new confidence into the members of the party, and the Corporal, uninvited, assumed command from that point, forming the prisoners into marching order, so that they quickened their pace.

About half a mile along the road, the challenge rang out in English from a sentry on duty guarding a munitions dump. It was answered by the startled Padre with a more than normal emphasis on the word 'Friend'. Seeking information from the sentry concerning the whereabouts of a 'cage' for the prisoners, he was directed to a place about a quarter of a mile still further along the road, and this was reached in a few minutes. The party halted, and the Padre advanced to a small wooden hut containing the friendly and hospitable light of candles. Standing at the door in the semi-darkness, the Padre noticed that the man in charge was a sergeant of the military police, a most important and influential member of the community. He responded to the footsteps in a voice that only such a creature can command, without even looking up.

'Hullo! Who's that?'
'I've a batch of prisoners, seventeen of them, to hand over to you, Sergeant.'
'Damned late aren't you? Bring 'em along 'ere.'

The Padre withdrew slightly to allow the prisoners to enter. But through the door of the hut he was greeted with:

'Halt there! What the devil do you think I'm going to do with 'em in 'ere? Who's in charge of this gang?'
'I am, Sergeant.'
'And who the ... are you? Step 'ere!'

The Padre complied without comment, and in the gloaming his identity was recognised. An apology was offered, though it seemed to lack sincerity as it was veiled by a smile. It was accepted with an even broader one.

'Where is the escort, Sir?'
'There is none, unless you'd like to call me one.'
'Who then shall I make out the receipt to, Sir?'
'There is no need for a receipt, as long as you will relieve me of this lot.'
'But, Sir, we must give a receipt when we take them over. It's orders.'
'Make it out to me then.'

So it was, and the exchange being completed, the Padre went away with his little chit for seventeen German prisoners. He set out to find his way back, but had not gone so far as to be out of hearing distance of the remark from inside – 'That was ... funny, Bill, wasn't it?' A hearty laugh rang out inside the hut, but the Padre felt entitled to join in, as heartily as anyone within, for he was feeling more thankful than at any other time in his life.

Although perhaps glad enough to part, both the prisoners and their 'guard' had learned something about each other. Sharing an ordeal like this had removed much of whatever it was that had destined them to be on opposite sides in a conflict. As a reward for their mutual trust, they were now so placed that, at least for 'the duration', they would not have to regard one another as enemies.

Chapter 13

A German Service

When a man faces an enemy who is armed and occupying a trench a few hundred yards away, he has no incentive to entertain kind thoughts concerning him. The fact that, at any moment, the command to attack would set them at each other with bared bayonets in a life and death struggle, makes sound judgement of each other impossible. But should fate decide that the German becomes the prisoner of the Britisher, then as soon as he is disarmed he is no longer treated as an enemy.

The Padre had new opportunities for getting to know individual Germans, since he was thrown into contact with them in the work they were called upon to do behind the lines.[1] He had to admit that there was a bigger common denominator in character than he had expected, and that differences were largely due to impressions given second-hand by others. At the hospital to which the Padre was attached for duty, he had opportunities for arranging religious services and these were apparently appreciated, as they were supported by both patients and staff in encouraging numbers. One day, as he was posting up on the notice board the arrangements for the Sunday, he was watched closely by a German prisoner who was doing duty in the scullery quarters. As soon as the Padre had left, this man carefully read the announcement and waited for an opportunity to speak to the Padre. In good English, albeit with a distinctively German accent, he enquired: 'Sir! Would any of us Germans be allowed to attend that service? A few of us can understand English well enough to follow and we should like to come.' 'Of course you can' was the answer suggested by instinct, but the Padre hesitated as he realised that granting this seemingly legitimate privilege was not as straightforward a matter as all that. But he did not want to reveal any obvious reluctance. He was glad of the

---

1 For photographs of German prisoners transporting supplies and repairing a road, see Carter, pp. 167, 171, 225.

opportunity of a few minutes for reflection, and side-tracked the issue with the enquiry:

'How long is it since you attended a service?'
'More than a year, Sir! Months before we were captured, things were so desperately hard for us that we had no opportunity at all. Since we have been prisoners we have never thought of any unusual privileges being granted. We should like to come, Sir!'

'Um!' was all the Padre could give as a reply just then, other than a promise to see what could be done about it.

Official religion forbade private ruling on a matter like this. Military regulations definitely banned fraternising with the enemy, for any reason. An act of worship involved men in something far deeper than mere fraternising – in friendly fellowship; therefore it seemed that the Padre had practically no hope of ever getting any further with the request. However, he decided to face the issue and as soon as possible make enquiries in the proper quarter. All this passed through his mind in a few seconds, but as he made ready to answer, his eyes met those of the German. A long steady enquiring gaze reaffirmed his belief that he knew the man from previous acquaintance. Still glad of a further delay, he said:

'Have you ever spoken to me before, Fritz? You are a Corporal, I see!'
'I think I have, Sir! Was it not you who a few months ago had a number of us prisoners stretcher-bearing after the Battle of Ypres? I was asked to help you when we were "lost" on our way back.'
'Are you the Corporal who acted as interpreter for me?'
'I am, Sir.'
'Well, well!'

The sudden remembrance of the profound gratitude he had felt on that occasion when he accepted the services offered, made the Padre, before he knew what he was doing, offer his hand and give the German an unmistakable comrade's grip. He was glad, however, when he had given it, to find that such a demonstration of friendliness was unobserved by anyone else!

It would have been quite excusable had that unexpected incident driven the real matter in hand into the background, and been a fitting farewell to one another, but the parting words of the German were: 'Sir! You will make that enquiry for us? When shall we know the result?' As anticipated, it was the soldier's point of view that was considered by the

Commanding Officer to whom the Padre took the matter. 'Regulations', Numbers this and that, were quoted with a definitiveness that seemed fatal. The C.O. marshalled arguments of every kind to show how unreasonable the request was. 'Usually', he said, 'there are nurses present at the services and their susceptibilities must be considered.' He spoke with an air of satisfied chivalry that unmistakably showed him to be in sympathy with the Regulations. He did want it to be understood, however, that he, as an individual, had no 'personal objection', but the rules must stand. Argument or persuasion being useless, the Padre withdrew, putting out of his mind once and for all the idea of a united service.

The German Corporal did not seem at all surprised at the decision. He had apparently anticipated it, for immediately he had learnt what it was he followed up with:

> 'Then is it possible for us to have one of our own?'
> 'If you have anyone to take charge I do not think there will be any objection, Corporal.'
> 'But could you not conduct it for us, Sir?'
> 'I hardly think so. My knowledge of German is so small that an attempt to do so on my part would be hopeless.'
> 'I would gladly act as your interpreter again, Sir!'

The offer was accompanied by a smile.

> 'My men are very keen about it, and we have talked about it since I told them I had mentioned it to you. We are often talking religion after we have finished for the day. We would like to know where God comes in, in this War, and a few things like that.'

The Padre could do no other than agree.

An arrangement was made whereby the manuscript of a brief sermon was presented to the Corporal on Thursday evening, and by Sunday it had been translated into his mother tongue. Following the service for the British staff, the Padre conducted one for the German prisoners only. He led the devotions in slow English, then by the aid of badly mutilated pigeon-German he introduced his subject, and then handed over the discourse to the interpreter who gave it from his elaborate manuscript. There was a slight feeling of uneasiness on the part of the Padre, since he was entirely at the mercy of the reader who might have used the occasion for propagandist purposes entirely unrelated to the Gospel. However, the good order, and the apparent appreciation of the listeners, dismissed the idea of treachery as unworthy of a Britisher. For three Sundays this procedure was adopted, but a further redistribution of troops took the Padre into another area and as far as he ever learned the practice was discontinued.

Chapter 14

Victory Hymns

In just a week, and once again it would be that day on the calendar when large congregations had through the centuries gathered to join in the singing of

> Hark the Herald Angels sing
> Glory to the Newborn King.
> Peace on earth and mercy mild,
> God and sinner reconciled ...

This year, however, the congregations would be smaller. There were fewer to sing, less to sing about, and a dearth of the thrilling experiences that put songs into the mouths of would-be singers.[1]

In a home at Blythespont sat a man and his wife at the fireside, and both gazed thoughtfully into the grate.[2] On Christmas Day, for many, many years the huge Yule log had thrown out its heat till the happy folk enjoying its warmth were forced to retire to a greater distance from the fire. However hot it might be this year, it would bring no cheer to Jim, for he was where blazing fires were not allowed and where he would have to content himself with the muffler and gloves knitted at that fireside – and with a few peppermints sent in the fortnightly parcel. A conversation was ventured on a topic not often introduced.

---

1 The connection between the two sections of this chapter (also a single chapter in the typescript), inadequately expounded and at best tenuous, is the singing at Christmas, in Britain and in France, of two hymns of victory over death. However, the reference to 'Jim', apparently a prodigal son, and his misdeeds the previous Christmas, seemingly his going on a spree while on leave and staying out all night to enjoy drink and sex, remains inept. Perhaps there was more about Jim in an earlier version or an abandoned chapter – perhaps that he was killed in the Christmas offensive of the following year.
2 'Blythespont' is unidentified and perhaps an invented name.

'It won't be much of a Christmas this year, Joe, with Jim out there, poor lad!'

'He'll make himself at home and be happy anywhere, and some of his pals will get the benefit of his capers. You will be wise, dear, not to dwell overmuch on things as they are to be this year.'

'True enough. Perhaps they'll have a happy Christmas. I don't see how anyone could help it with Jim there. Anyway what happened last year will not happen again this year, will it?'

'No.'

'I've thought a lot about the anxiety we had then, when for the first time we had to reconcile ourselves to the fact that home was not as much to him as it had been. I've never found out where he got to, have you?'

'No. But it is no use reliving those hours; they are over and done with now, and since then we have had nothing to complain of in Jim. Forget it, dear, and make the best of the good things still left to us.'

'I suppose though, in the trenches men are safe from the kind of temptation we were so concerned about?'

'Quite. War's a serious business right enough but it does discipline men and save them from some things. We must think of him doing his bit there even on a Christmas day, and that will have some compensations for both him and us.'

'Perhaps so.'

Both resumed their activities, one darning and the other reading his paper.

'Any better news today?' asked the woman later.

'About the same. Things won't happen for a bit now. Winter is no time for "offensives"; we have that consolation.'

'Is that always so?'

'Generally, dear.'

With a feeling of partial relief, the woman settled again to her darning and the man to his reading.

★★★

Almost synchronising with this conversation was the movement of the reserve troops going up to occupy that part of the line which had been vacated by our attacking troops, who had not only reached their objective but were pushing on to complete their success with a distinctive thrust into the enemy line. Theories concerning winter operations, and sentiments associated with a special date on the almanac, were unreliable data upon which to work. At this point in the campaign, things happened just when and how they liked. Men had to make the best of things as they found them. A further attack on the enemy position was contemplated and in view of the recent success it looked as though it could be attempted on a grand scale. But in December it would be a costlier business than at a more ideal time of the year.³

The Padre of the regiment, by now an old hand in actual warfare, fully realised that there would be a call upon his services, and he judged that he could be of most value on the roads immediately behind the advancing troops. He had a long enough experience to know how valuable are the few minutes immediately following a casualty, when often the man's very life depends upon speedy and efficient first aid. Not a few men owed their survival to his aid at such times when they were almost despairing in the attempt to deal with their newly inflicted wounds.⁴ And he was grateful for the opportunity to translate Christian theories into practical ministries. He had overtaken the reserve troops and passed on to the road leading up to the attack. His first call was to give a few minutes, for that was all that was needed, to a man lying at the roadside who had fallen a victim to the shell-fire of the enemy guns as it searched the approaches to the front line. Then, raising himself and replacing his cap on his bared head, he set out again.

Almost immediately he met a man hobbling back, dragging a badly wounded foot along the ground. The Padre's offer to re-dress it was declined with the remark that it was comfortable. In fact, an oft-encircling puttee held in place a soft sodden forage cap, which in turn kept a first aid pad over a hole in the foot, the puttee thus doing service as a bandage. While resting a short time at the spot, the Padre saw another man groping his way back with the help of a comrade. The latter handed over his charge at the invitation of the Padre. Offering an outstretched arm to the first wounded man, the Padre set off towards the dressing-

---

3 The December of a new offensive (with Jim in France at Christmas) must be that of 1917, since Rider only returned to the war front as a Padre in January 1917. But December 1917 had no new offensive. British success in the Battle of Cambrai earlier in the year had been followed by a successful German counter-attack, and December saw only both sides licking their wounds. Rider must have confused the date.
4 This is the closest Rider gets to mentioning the episode of his own rescuing of wounded men under fire which earned him the award of the Military Cross.

station with a blinded man and a lamed man, one on each arm, as his companions.[5]

In a large dugout at the side of a sunken road, a little behind the lines, was an efficient Advanced Dressing-Station, whose staff were busy preparing for another big 'show'. The Padre took up his post here. It was only when the guns announced the zero hour that the busy R.A.M.C.[6] men gave themselves a short respite for relaxation. However, although they had done more than one might have expected with the small medical resources at their disposal, they were scarcely satisfied with the arrangements made. The offer of the Padre's assistance in the less skilled work of the 'station' was readily accepted by the doctors, and soon he was busy binding up minor wounds, and helping with the evacuation of the patients ready for conveyance still further back, towards the Base. For hours this strenuous work had to be carried out, and the strain was taking its toll on the strength of the R.A.M.C. staff, yet, until the rush was over, there was no possibility of their even working in shifts. With the agreement of the surgeons, who, on an improvised operating table were compelled in many instances to complete the amputations begun by shell fragments, he found ample opportunity for assisting. He held the broken limbs in position as they were being put into splints; he learned how to administer anaesthetics and to watch for the signs that registered their effectiveness; and he occasionally worked to support those with respiratory emergencies. For instance, he was called upon to hold the head and arms of patients who had to submit to the terrible pain of having their broken thighs pulled into position for placing in a Thomas's splint.[7] Abundant proof was given that men can be superlatively courageous when circumstances of suffering demand that they should be.[8]

---

5 Possibly this episode is highlighted because of its Christian resonances. The blind and the lame are regularly linked in the Bible and Jesus made 'the blind see and the lame walk' (Luke 7:23).
6 Royal Army Medical Corps
7 This form of splint for all fractures of the leg above the calf, invented by H.O. Thomas and brought into general use by his nephew, Sir Robert Jones, was extensively used in World War I.
8 For similar accounts of a chaplain at an A.D.S., organising transport of the wounded and dead and at least on one occasion actually assisting in the medical work ('dawn found us still at it, bandaging, dressing, putting cases away to the Casualty Clearing Station as soon as possible'), see *Bickersteth* JB, pp. 106, 220. Earlier in the war, Chaplain Doundney, who had had some medical experience in backwoods Australia, helped with the wounded, 'mostly to assist the surgeon' (Horne, *Doundney*, p. 160). Methodist Chaplain Watkins, who in the first months of the war was attached to a field ambulance, recounted many scenes at dressing-stations (Watkins, *With French*, passim).

The attack that had been launched with costly success had involved a brigade of South Africans, among whose men were many fine specimens of swarthy manhood. A fine, big, jet-black South African was brought in on a stretcher, and a mere glance at him revealed the fact that he had been badly knocked about in the battle. From the first he looked a hopeless case, yet all that could be done for him, in the faint hope that his life could be saved, was done by the sympathetic doctors. When he was carried away after treatment he had only one leg and no forearms and was like an embalmed body, so swathed in bandages was he, almost from head to foot. Yet still he lived and was conscious through it all, but obviously quite unfit for evacuation down the line, over the rough roads and in the hard transport that at such times had to do duty as ambulances.

The doctor had seen that the stretcher on which the poor man lay was taken to the far end of the dugout and placed in a quiet, dark corner, where it was left to the after-care of the Padre. In the faint glow of the light from two candles, he sat by the stretcher, listening to the faint remarks of the patient, some of which were enquiries, and others were expressions of gratitude for attention received. In about forty minutes, welcome sleep visited the patient and the Padre rejoined the staff of doctors. They were still busy in the other part of the dugout but were preparing to relax from their labours, as only a few minor casualties were by now needing attention. The Padre paid frequent visits to the mutilated man at the far end and was comforted by the fact that he was still sleeping. The simple, quiet ministrations of the grace of God were asked for, and the man was left to what was anticipated as a peaceful 'passing'. There was some movement, not so much of muscles, but like the agitation of the soul as it attempted to withdraw itself from the poor body; and the Padre left the man to pass out and 'enjoy death'.

Three of the doctors were sitting down, grateful for the easing up of their toil, and were disinterestedly partaking of tea and biscuits at the hour of three a.m. Then, in the deep silence, faint but clear strains of a song came from out of the darkness at the end of the dugout, where, it was assumed, there lay, by then, the dead body of the South African. All activity ceased for a few moments; it seemed sacrilegious to do anything but listen. Everyone felt conscious of a 'presence'. As the song continued it became clearer, and was easily distinguishable as the rendering of two complete verses of 'Jesu, Lover of my soul'. Quietly the Padre stole along to the singer, and in the dim light of the now spluttering candle he stood by him, and watched him slowly sink as the last verse, in fainter and fainter tones, was slowly completed:

Safe into the haven guide,
O receive my soul at last.⁹

Only the movement of his lips announced how far he had got with his 'victory song'. Further verses of the hymn he would complete in a more triumphant strain as he entered the choir stalls in the Temple of God, for he passed over with music in his soul and a smile on his face.

The doctors were obviously impressed that God had stolen into their sanctuary of healing. Surely it was true that He visited them, as an acknowledgement of their faithful service. God associates Himself with any ministry of love, no matter where it is performed; and one does well to assume the likelihood of the presence of God even on a battlefield. God who knew what it was to humble himself and lay his glory by, had come down even lower than usual, to share the travail of those of his servants who worked in a vile atmosphere, where the exhalations of over two hundred wounded men and their dripping wounds had fouled everything within reach.

After this, binding up the broken men in that dugout was regarded as something more than just a duty – it had become a sacrament. Next day, the Padre's duties took him back to the Casualty Clearing Station, a larger place where the wounded from many sectors had been taken, and where the magnitude of the attack and its cost could better be estimated. The entire staff of nurses had been on duty all night, washing the filth from wounds, and administering oxygen in the attempt to tide over a period of despair and weakness in some poor man, even if he had only an infinitesimal chance of recovery; or trying to assist a man who was 'frothing up' and well-nigh choking in the after-stages of a gas attack.¹⁰ And finally, when they had to acknowledge that all their efforts had been unsuccessful, as they went round the stretchers and beds, here and there they pulled a blanket higher up to cover a man's face, an indication that their services were not required any longer. A witness of such amazing endurance and service could have only profound admiration.

---

9 The first verse of this still popular hymn reads as follows. 'Jesu, lover of my soul, / Let me to your bosom fly, / While the gathering waters roll, / While the tempest still is nigh. / Hide me, O my Saviour, hide, / Till the storm of life is past; / Safe into the haven guide, / O receive my soul at last.' Possibly an additional attraction of this anecdote for Rider was that the hymn was composed by Charles Wesley, the founder of Methodism. Rider, however, slipped up in referring to the 'complete two verses' and to the 'last verse', when he meant 'complete two lines' and 'last line'.
10 Wilfred Owen was particularly revolted by the gas casualties; e.g., ' ... the blood / Comes gurgling from the froth-corrupted lungs' ('Dulce et decorum est').

There were other calls upon the ministries of God. In some parts of the battlefield where any attempt at rescue work was too dangerous, men were still lying out on the ground, using perhaps a shell hole or the spot where they had fallen as the 'Waiting Room' to their 'Resting Place'. For them, the only possible consolations and 'last rites' had to be performed by God Himself, as He hallowed the ground that had been the scene of the cruel havoc of battle, and made it into a place where great men 'Lie in State'. That ministering spirits had been busy could be judged from the smiles that lightened the faces of many men even in death, and gave one the impression that they had heard the 'Well done!' that makes everything worth while.

Busy days were to follow for the Padre. There fell to him the task of searching the battlefield for the 'fallen', identifying them and taking any personal belongings which had a sentimental value (and there was seldom anything else), to be sent to the home address of those who would prize them most.[11] Carefully marking the spots where the dead lay, he made arrangements for burial as soon as it was possible. For this task, he attached himself to an officer who, with six men, bearing the exalted status of a 'Burial Party', were detailed to collect bodies and inter them. Part of an unwanted trench had been chosen as the cemetery, and in it thirty bodies had been reverently laid side by side. All was ready for the brief Committal Service and the whole company stood bareheaded as the Padre proceeded. These activities had been spotted by a German observer who, presumably not knowing the real purpose of the work, had reported troop movements to his artillery commander. With incredible smartness and accuracy of aim, a salvo of high-velocity shells arrived in quick succession, almost on the very burial spot. Forced to take hurried cover, the whole party, having no alternative, fell headlong into the trench upon the mutilated and already decomposing bodies that had been so reverently placed there a few minutes before. In war, a very thin line divides the 'quick' from the 'dead'. During the lull that followed the men sorted themselves out from their less fortunate brothers, and crawled over the edge of the grave to run for cover in a short section of a sunken road near by, leaving the 'filling-in' to be done later, after dark.[12] The work was com-

---

11 In July 1916, on the Somme, Bickersteth and another chaplain identified the dead. 'We removed all personal property and placed it in a sack, and identified the body by the identification disc or pay book, and then marked it carefully by writing details on the label and tying the label to the coat or tunic, and then passed on to the next' (Bickersteth JB, p. 109).

12 Chaplain Bickersteth and a work party also had to take cover in a mass grave when shelled, but one not yet containing bodies (*Bickersteth* JB, p. 111).

pleted that night by the burial party, but the Padre was sitting by the light of smoking candles, writing. Thirty letters, with almost as many packages of personal effects found on the bodies of the fallen – photographs, letters, cuttings and many other things including simple 'charms'[13] – all to be despatched to the homes of the next-of-kin to which the loved one would never return.[14]

13 The contents of the emptied pockets of a deserter about to be shot included 'a lucky farthing' which his sweetheart had given him and which he arranged to be returned, with other personal effects, to her (*Bickersteth* JB, p. 224).
14 Cf. 'We have, I fear, in my battalion over 400 missing ... I have traced 300 wounded ... The task of writing to their people is quite beyond me, and I do not know how to write to those whose dear ones are missing' (*Bickersteth* JB, p. 110).

Chapter 15

Horses and Refugees

A new driver had been sent to the battery. He brought limited qualities to commend him to his pals. He had the nickname 'Fiz', suggestively given to him because of its unlikely association with his generous avoirdupois. He had a big heart matching his massive frame, and when he was in a fit condition to control the latter's expression, he could meet any demand made upon him. He was a most unusual character, a strange mixture of many and varied soul qualities. At times he was bold to the point of absolute defiance, at other times he was ridiculously shy. Occasionally he would reveal a surprising graciousness of spirit in contrast to his customary clumsiness. He was particularly good to a pair of horses entrusted to his care, and they were always in fine condition when turned out for duty under all circumstances, easy or gruelling, as though for a 'show'. He had the distinction of always having the best pair of leaders in the Brigade, yet he would often be reproved for his own unsoldierly appearance. Late on parade innumerable times, it was ever his excuse that Bess and Joey had got very dirty and it had taken him much longer to groom them.

He was a bit of a problem to the Padre. He would change as often and as completely in his moods as an April day. One moment he could be relied upon like a trusted friend; the next moment there was reason for the greatest anxiety; one day a saint, the next a hardened sinner. His actions would furnish illustrations of almost any virtue and any vice, save that his greatest enemy could never accuse him of deliberate and premeditated corruption or disloyalty. Nothing better pleased the Padre than to get him to 'open out' on any matter he felt inclined to mention, for no one else ever made such a unique if bizarre contribution to the subject.

Great excitement prevailed one day when the Brigade received orders from Headquarters to proceed at once and with all speed to another part of the line. It was to what had been regarded as a particularly quiet sector where for some time the troops of another of the Allied Armies had been stationed to hold the line. This, however, they had failed to do, and a surprise attack made by the enemy on a substantial front had resulted in a decided breach in the Allied line. Two British divisions were rushed up to fill it.[1]

This unexpected thrust had disturbed very considerably the state of things in the area just behind the line in that sector of the front. The previous comparative calm and security of things there had lured a few of the peasant population to re-establish themselves on their farms, and they had been working bravely there for many months, within sound of the enemy guns. In one large village, just out of range of the enemy light artillery fire, many refugees from further afield, fleeing at the time of the first advance of the Germans two and a half years earlier, had decided to halt and stay, in the belief that it would be a matter of a few days only before they could return home.[2] Instead, very many months passed with no change in the battlefront. Then, one day, the sudden thrust by the Germans brought more refugees, and with them many wild, half-true rumours of further enemy advance. This created a scare mentality. Moreover, enemy shells began to fall in the streets of the village, causing many casualties among the civilians. The evacuation of the entire community became necessary and orders to that effect were issued. Soon the roads were thronged with the once-ejected and now twice-ejected peasants of the stricken land, a sorry spectacle even for the war-hardened Tommies to witness. The latter soon realised what a blessing the existence of the English Channel was to their own loved ones.

An amount of ground had been taken from the Allies as a result of the German attack, and in the panic and unexpected flight, two Belgian girls,

---

1 This refers to a Portuguese division on 9–10 April 1918, on the Lys front, during the final German major offensive (J.E. Edmonds, *Military Operations. France and Belgium 1918 (March–April)*, London, 1937, pp. 165–8). 'These troops were undoubtedly the worst of any nation in the West, and had always been regarded as utterly worthless' (Cruttwell, pp. 516–7). A fine monument in the main avenue of Lisbon records the Portuguese military contribution to the Great War; that 'the front line troops suffered heavy losses' (H.V. Livermore, *A New History of Portugal*, Cambridge, 1966, p. 327) is more discreet than exact. In fairness, the men were ill-equipped, poorly motivated, due relief, and distressed by the northern climate and ground conditions (as generously explained in Edmonds, *Military Operations 1918*, p. 187). The Portuguese rout occurred before Armentières, on the Franco-Belgium border, and the account says that Rider's Brigade was sent there to fill the gap. Part of the territory gained in the German attack and lost in the British counter-attack was in Belgium, hence the subsequent reference to two Belgian girls trapped in their home.

2 'Two and a half years earlier' would put the first German advance at autumn 1915; it was actually in autumn 1914, three and a half years earlier.

having lost contact with the other members of their family, had been left behind and had taken refuge in the cellar of their house, as a protection against shell-fire.[3] They had often sheltered this way before, and they hoped that there was nothing to distinguish this occasion from earlier ones, anticipating that in a few hours they could come out again and carry on with their duties. But the firing continued for a long time, and shell-fire gave place to rifle shots. They were caught up in a prolonged attack. Eventually things quietened down somewhat, and they stole up from their cellar-sanctuary, only to find rifle shooting going on intermittently all round the house. In the new dispositions of troops after the attack, it was situated in 'no-man's-land' and the girls discovered that they were trapped. They fled again into the cellar, too terrified to stir. There they remained imprisoned for three days. Then followed indications of renewed battle, which they correctly interpreted as an allied counter-attack. Whatever the consequences of this new activity, they felt slightly relieved by the thought that it might result in their liberation.

For three hours there was incessant firing, and some of the shells burst very near to them, near enough to scar the walls of the house and to shake the loose mortar from the underground walls. One particularly heavy explosion made their home rock, and they believed that their hiding place was going to become their tomb. They were famished, cold and panic-stricken. They huddled together at the far end of the cellar, holding each other tightly and relaxing only a little between the bursts of fire. After a further two hours of conflict there was quiet, and they pondered what to do. Hearing no dangerous sounds, they decided to venture up the steps again, but when they did so at first could see nothing. They were contemplating coming out into the open when they heard sounds of approaching horses and transport, so hurriedly withdrew, closing the door above them.

The British infantry had retaken the lost ground and were advancing beyond the house, while the field artillery had been ordered to bring up a single gun and position it at the farm, in order to harass the retreating Germans. As the girls cowered below, in the yard above stood three pairs of horses harnessed to a gun limber. The dismounted drivers, sharing a packet of 'Trumpeters' and puffing away happily, listened to one of their number describing the virtues of his 'pair of beauties'. After what seemed an eternity to them, although it could not have been more than two hours, the imprisoned girls decided to try to get a glimpse of what was taking

---

3 For 'Belgian girls', see note 1 of the present chapter.

place above them. Slowly they pushed open the door a few inches and held it in position by wedging it with a piece of fallen stone. Peering through the opening, they were at first blinded by the light and could see nothing. When their eyes had become accustomed to it, they could make out the form of horses, but at first were not able to discern whether the drivers were members of the German or Allied armies. They looked for familiar clues in their dress, but the men were wearing different uniforms from those worn by the men who until a few days before had been billeted at their farm. Whoever they were, the only course seemed to be to venture forth. They slowly lifted the door a little at a time. This attracted the attention of the driver with his 'beauties', and he kept his surprised eyes glued to the spot. Noticing two human faces and thinking they might be those of Germans, he prepared himself for any emergency. But the human forms, emerging from the cellar and seeing his suspicious movements, instantly threw themselves into his arms, literally, in an appeal for mercy.

Fiz, for such it was, recoiled and stared at them in utter bewilderment, too nonplussed either to speak or act. They began to gesticulate wildly, while using a language that was unintelligible to him. Still clinging tightly to his arms, they eventually made it clear that they were imploring him to do something. What could he do? He had no idea – the poor things were so hungry and terrified that they seemed almost as if they were attacking him. An enemy shell dropped near, scaring the girls still more, and waving their arms they conveyed to him that they were asking him what direction to take to escape. Fiz, relieved that their whole intention was to leave him, pointed in the direction of the road along which he had come. But as the fugitives ran down it, he stared after them through tear-stained eyes. He was aroused from his reverie by the command 'Mount!', and he climbed into his stirrups and was soon astride his horse. 'Advance!' was the signal to move off, and he was glad to be away from the emotional encounter.

Shedding tears was something Fiz never remembered having done before in his life. As he turned a corner, he glanced back along the road and saw the appealing faces of the girls looking back for more advice. This he gave by waving his whip and pointing again in the direction they were going. Another bursting shell sent the girls diving for safety and the smoke screened them from his further gaze. 'Poor devils! Gawd 'elp 'em!' This was all he could say as he tried to swallow a big lump in his throat, and he spurred his horses to carry him away.

He would not have called his utterance a prayer, but such it was, and it had all the sincerity that made it effectual. It was answered by the

Sergeant Cook of an infantry battalion that was coming into the line, inasmuch as he ordered its travelling kitchen to halt by the roadside, in the shelter of a few stumps of trees. Seeing the girls' sorry plight as they approached, yet knowing nothing of the nightmare through which they had passed, he recognised only slowly their appeal to his compassion. But the troops were so surprised and delighted to see females after their long separation from such that they did not hesitate to offer them hospitality of the kind they wanted. The two parties soon sensed the situation and in a few moments hungry Tommies and two famished Belgian girls were sharing the delicious stew from the kitchen. A little ready wit brightened the occasion, even though some of it was crude. But tears were near the surface, and they showed themselves a little later, at the separation that sent the girls seeking shelter at God knows where, and the men to do God knows what.

Fiz and his companions had taken their gun into position, and had set out with the empty limber on the return journey, the horses trotting merrily, knowing, as horses do, that their heads were homewards. Fiz had recovered somewhat from his emotional storm of two hours before and, as he passed within a hundred yards of the scene of bewilderment in the farmyard, he was able to gaze at it again in quieter mood. He was still very involved and concerned because of the plight of the two girls whom he had so unexpectedly met there, and he scanned the road along which they had gone, but only the ordinary associations with a front-line area were to be seen. The darkness was beginning to fall and there was limited vision.

A momentarily announced approach of a large shell made the team hesitate and crouch, and the next second there was confusion as the shell exploded and one of the horses in the leading pair was hit. The driver unhitched his pair and handed over the sound horse to the other drivers, hoping to be able to comply with his sergeant's order to bring along his wounded horse in his own time and report his arrival at the 'lines'. He made the attempt, but his wounded charge collapsed, and lay in a heap in the road. A quarter of an hour later, an officer was making his way along the road when he was arrested by hearing rather strange words: 'Joey, my beauty! Poor devil! Gawd 'elp yer!' The officer found Fiz kneeling by his horse with its head on his lap, obviously distressed by the absence of any of the usual responses to his caressings. Shining his flash lamp on the strange heap, the officer challenged whoever or whatever it was.

'Friend!', came in reply.

'Well, man, What is the trouble?'

'My old pal 'ere 'as got it bad. Shoot the poor devil out of his misery, Sir, will you?'

The officer carefully looked round and found the dying horse with an ugly wound in its side. A revolver shot rang out in the stillness and the officer moved on.

The lone figure of Fiz carrying a spare harness over his shoulder – and with a heavy heart beneath his tunic – entered the lines soon after nine o'clock. The day's life had been full of incident, revealing to Fiz the fact that there were things harder to bear than wounds. Twice within a few hours his soul had been over-weighted and softened; now without his pal he thought life could never be the same again. After a drink of tea, he sat down by a brazier fire, musing. Staring into the glow his mind travelled again to the scenes of the earlier evening and pictured again the two half-demented girls in their distress. He also wondered at his own perplexity when faced with the situation in which they had figured, for he could not recall being at any time before at a loss in the presence of females. Perhaps it was their novel attitude to him. The manner in which they had trusted him and had counted on his protection was very different from the girls of his acquaintance – they never took any liberties with him as they considered him incapable of chivalry. He unconsciously broke the silence with: 'Poor devils! Gawd 'elp 'em!' 'Cheer up, old fellow! You are darned quiet this evening', remarked his companion, who was the driver to whom he had handed over his unwounded horse. 'You ain't the only chap what's lost 'is 'oss.' There was no reply, so his companion, hoping to induce him to sing as he had so often done before, struck up 'There's a long, long road a-winding into the land of my dreams'. But it was a solo effort, so he stopped, and inviting another of his chums to join him, they set off together into the night.

The Padre had turned in, and he got into conversation with Fiz who rewarded his interest by giving him his own version of the events of the evening in the limited but vivid language at his command. Conversation then became general and a little later it had become quite intimate, as Fiz started talking about the people at home. But at this point they were interrupted. 'Stoke up, me 'earties, get the dixie lid going!' This call came from two excited men who had broken into the proceedings without first noticing what was taking place inside the billet. They were carrying six large juicy steaks and were preparing to have a right good 'tuck in'. Said the Padre:

'My word, they look good, lads! I'd better get off before I break the commandment about coveting.'

'You can 'ave one, Sir, if you like', came the reply.

'Thank you, lads! But I'll leave you to enjoy them as I shall get my supper presently. Now tuck in and have a good time. Good luck to you!'

'Good night, Sir!'

The Padre went into the darkness. Little did he suspect at the time that the chops had been part of Joey's carcass a few minutes before.

Men whose hunger rather than their tastes decided when a thing was good had no aversion to a bit of good horseflesh. Yet there was no horse in the unit that had been better cared for than this particular one. At first Fiz was not a bit interested in this act of sacrilege. When, however, there was a sizzling sound, accompanied by a rich appetising smell, all this proved to be too big a temptation to his inner man for him to resist, and he did his bit to see that the meal which memorialised an old pal was worthy of the occasion.

Being a good soldier, he had learned to put trouble behind him, and the next day he began the long process of making a pal of the new horse given him to replace Joey. It was, unfortunately, a case of 'being unequally yoked', and the old sentimental trinity of companionship between horses and driver was never fully re-established. However, the experiences that day had softened the nature of Fiz, and in future he was a more agreeable workmate with his human friends.

Chapter 16

Liberation

The advance during the later stages of the War was so rapid that the conquering troops entered villages before the civilians had had time to evacuate them, with the result that the troops had to be billeted on the peasant population, at least for the night. On these occasions, the Padre, with two N.C.O.s, went forward to make the necessary arrangements. Often his little company represented the first troops to enter after the retiring Germans had passed through a village and had carried away with them most of the village's stock of foodstuffs.[1] Anticipating still more enemy troops, the villagers received the newcomers with their normal hostile and cold greetings, and daring little boys even ran out to spit at the party and then dash indoors again. Since he was not recognised as a Padre, old men and women scowled and frowned when he approached them. However, because new and gentler methods of contact were employed than those to which they had become accustomed, this gave some credence to the rumours they had heard that 'the English were coming'. The women gathered in groups and began to whisper to one another, now and again casting a furtive glance at one or other of the trio of strangers. Soon their instinctive judgement removed all suspicion, and they came forward with eloquent gestures of help. By the time the troops arrived for their quarters, doubt had been dispelled and shyness conquered. With appropriate joyousness the villagers began celebrations, making the most of the scanty resources available, despite their larders being empty and their reserves almost nil.

The good news of the arrival of 'liberating troops' sped ahead of the advancing columns and the billeting party had the benefit of this previ-

---

1 As suggested in note 54 of the introduction, Rider's accompanying the forward party of a British advance may indicate that he was, on this occasion, with the infantry rather than the artillery.

ous announcement. As soon as they entered later villages, a host of grateful peasants began to shower their affections upon the embarrassed members of the party. The Padre found himself surrounded in the roadway and being freely kissed by the women and girls and even old men, whose weeping eyes wet his own cheeks as well as theirs. This was an alarming demonstration for Britishers, with their usual antipathy to emotional profusion of any kind, and it made them rather poor recipients of this form of gratitude. The urgency of their billeting work was a good excuse for a welcome escape from strong emotion.

In one village, the Padre, engaged on the same work, entered what appeared to be an uninhabited though furnished house, and in it he came across an old lady lying on straw in the kitchen, fast asleep. Without disturbing her, but wondering whether she was ill or had been the victim of some misfortune, he stole upstairs to make further investigations. There he found two double beds showing signs of recent occupation and abandoned in a state of disorder. When he descended the stairs, the woman had roused herself and was fearfully and unresistingly awaiting what she imagined to be her fate. Instead, she was greeted with a friendly *'bonjour'*, which seemingly was such a surprise that she could not answer. Soon she was assured that the ownership of the house had been restored to her, and all that was required was somewhere for a few troops to sleep. She indicated the upstairs rooms, saying that they had been slept in by troops for over three weeks, and since she herself had the straw in the kitchen she was provided for. For more than one reason, this offer was not accepted, and the old lady was told that there would be no further interference in her home. Her gratitude at this news caused her to go to her heap of straw to uncover what she had hidden there, a small store of potatoes. She began to peel these and offered to prepare them for the three men who were standing by her empty grate. Again her offer was not accepted, once it was learned that she had had nothing but potatoes for three days and that they were the only reserves of food left in the house.

Seen at the roadside as the party made its way towards another village the next day, was a little group consisting of an aged couple, and a younger mother with her two children, a girl and a boy each about ten years old. Overtaken in the darkness before they had been able to secure a shelter, they had spent the night all huddled together under the cover of a small cluster of trees in the neighbouring field. Now they were chewing the raw steaks they had cut from the carcass of a horse they had discovered, although it had been abandoned in the retreat of the Germans at least four days before. The man and the boy, having finished their meal, were again visiting the animal, to obtain more supplies for their journey. The man was cutting into the animal with a knife, while the boy was hacking at the remaining flesh with a sharp stone he had kicked out of the paved roadway. Stocked with their fresh supplies, they then set out along the road to an unknown destination.

The billeting party also saw a reminder of the price the British had paid in repatriating the villagers. Many dead Tommies were lying at the roadside. At the doorways of houses the residents had assembled to welcome the newcomers. But there was scarcely a single instance of any individual in a medical category higher than that of C.3. Those still in residence were mostly old men and women who had been too frail to make their escape and take to the road. There were also occasional worn and worried women with little children at their heels; the halt and blind too had stayed behind, and here and there the village imbecile, a half-witted fellow who greeted all that was happening with high glee. Yet all the victims of the fight were A.1 men. The Padre could not help reflecting that a heavy price had been paid for such a 'prize'. Even on the broadest interpretation of New Testament teaching, he felt that this scene was scarcely what the Master meant when he counselled the 'sacrifice of the strong for the weak'.[2]

Still in search of accommodation, the Padre descended a flight of steps leading below ground from the front door of a large house a little distance off the main thoroughfare. At the bottom, as he lit a match to give a momentary glimmer of light, he was startled by a call, in hoarse weak tones, of '*Kamarad! Kamarad!*' Lighting fresh matches, he peered into the darkness and saw six wounded German soldiers lying on the ground. The previous day, they had been placed within the house by their comrades who were fast in retreat, in order to receive medical attention at the hands of a doctor. But before anything could be done for them, the alarm was raised that the British were at the edge of the town, and the men had had to be abandoned. Fearful of what might happen to them, they had crawled down the cellar steps for safety, and had been there until the Padre arrived nearly twelve hours later. He saw their plight, and started to ascend the steps in the hope of securing assistance.

In doing this, he put his hand on the wall, and was much puzzled when it sank into a velvety, soft substance, the contact causing a weird buzzing sound to come from the place. Calling up the steps for the other men to

---

2 Not a Biblical quotation, but an extension of a Pauline theme, e.g. 'we agree to bear the burdens of the weak', Romans 15:1.

bring down their torch-lamps, he waited in the darkness till one was handed to him. Shining it on the spot about which he was so curious, he found the whole wall thickly covered with flies, which had swarmed there in tens of thousands. This phenomenon he associated more with an Eastern land than with France. Had it been the right time of the year, it might have answered the query about where these insects go in winter. Once the Germans were removed, the door was shut on that cellar, and the house was silently omitted from the official billeting list.

Chapter 17

Armistice[1]

The going had been difficult for weeks. The clever rear-guard action by the Germans had prepared a rough road for their pursuers. Demolition work had been thorough: roads were blown up, bridges destroyed and riverbanks pierced so as to flood the countryside. Worst of all, the roads were thronged with fleeing refugees, trudging ever Westward in the hope that eventually they would reach some hospitable and quiet resting place. This was a depressing spectacle for the Tommies, but their morale had been improved by what the 'movement' signified. They were able to sing as they marched, and dared even at times to break all the rules by handing their iron rations to the starving folk, ready to take the risk that things would not again make their use necessary for themselves.

The Padre of the unit, continuing to act as billeting officer, with a small section of two N.C.O.s, went forward every morning to where, according to orders, the next halt for the night's rest was to be made. He was on this errand on the morning of November 9th, 1918, when two mounted staff officers proceeding hurriedly along the road hailed him. 'Good morning, Padre! Great days these, eh?' Thinking that the remark was but a comment on fine weather, the Padre replied:

---

[1] This chapter appeared anonymously in the November 1957 issue of *The Old Contemptible*, under the title 'Armistice in the Field (1918)', and with the following introduction, probably not by the editor of the magazine since it reads very much as if by Rider himself. 'Time passes, lengthening the period between the end of the First World War and now, and memory alone can recapture the feelings we had when the "Cease Fire" brought to an end that phase of the campaign which had been the most exhilarating and rewarding of all ... the advance through the Hindenburg Line to what we had hoped was to be Berlin. Today the setting for Armistice celebrations is so different from those in the field, that there seems scarcely any connection between them. Because of this, a few Old Chums might be able to relive that period immediately preceding Eleven a.m., November 11th, 1918, by reading the following account of what happened in one small section on the Western Front.'

'They are, Sir! Where is Old Fritz now?'

'It matters little where he is now: it's where he will be in a day or two's time that interests us. The news this morning was that the Kaiser has abdicated.[2] Things will move quickly now. Cheerio!'

They galloped away with nothing to corroborate their statement save their eagerness to pass it on to others. The little party stood gazing at one another. Unable to assess the full significance of the news, they quietly returned to their work of billeting, seemingly unimpressed, perhaps unconvinced.

However, the news had reached the villagers. Until a few days before they had been sheltering from the Germans, who, in their state of semi-panic, had given little consideration to anything but their own escape. Emboldened by the rumour, old men and women and a few children made their way into the road, transfigured by a hope that they had seen the last of their unwelcome hosts of the last three years. They congregated in numbers much greater than had been permitted for many, many months, to talk and dream and trust. For a while they were hesitant about acceptance of the soldiers in uniforms unfamiliar to them, lest they should turn out to be other than British Tommies, but that fear once allayed, they gradually attempted to fraternise, with almost pathetic humility.

An old man had brought from his cellar an old chair and was sitting on the roadway by the ruins of his wrecked homestead.[3] The enemy had exploded a charge in the road to delay the advance of their pursuers, and the old man's house had shared the fate of the road. Sitting there thinking and waiting, he noticed that the limbers of the gun waggons and the men riding them were being given a bad shaking when they attempted to negotiate the hole in the road. He therefore busied himself, slowly carrying two at a time the bricks from his demolished walls, and filling in the hole, until after two hours he had the satisfaction of seeing that he had eased the strain on his new friends. Struggling again to his chair, he sat and mused and hoped.

By now the unit had reached the village where it was to rest for the night. The next morning, the billeting party was on the move to repeat

---

2 9 November 1918.

3 Among the proposed illustrations for his account, Rider included a photograph (apparently original) of a woman clambering over the wreckage of a house, and labelled it 'Home again (in Belgium)'.

the process of finding shelter in barns and sheds in another village, a few miles farther on the road to Germany. The road ascended the crest of a hill from which could be seen, less than ten miles away, a town of substantial proportions. Villagers assured the Padre that it was Mons, the place from which our Army had set out four years before on its unenviable retreat.[4]

The party was actively engaged in visiting houses and barns when the same two staff officers who had showed themselves two days before surprised it, by pulling up to speak to the Padre.

'Well, Padre, you can ease up a bit. You've heard the news?'
'No, Sir. What is it?'
'Well, it's all over at eleven o'clock this morning.'
'What is, Sir?'
'The whole ... war. It's 'Cease Fire' at 11.00 hours today.[5] Cheerio!'
'Cheerio, Sir!'

Within seconds the officers were out of sight, leaving three men staring at one another, bewildered, until after what seemed to be a long time, a smile crept across their faces suggesting that they were waking up to the fact that something really significant had finally happened.

However, the last orders having been to continue with the work of billeting, the party set itself to this until further orders were received. Somehow the task had lost its thrill. The excitement had cooled off and a feeling of limpness, a sense of lost purpose, made them feel they had been uncontrollably translated into a new kind of life. In the village there was an atmosphere of subdued emotion. Almost the entire population was silently making its way to the church, whose merrily ringing bells were a sufficient confirmation of the rumour to warrant the act of thanksgiving.

Soon the unit arrived. The villagers thought that its early arrival would give the opportunity to 'celebrate'. But the men were halted by the roadside, while the battalion cooks got busy with the mobile kitchens to provide an unhurried hot meal for them. No order came to occupy the billets. Instead, the order that came was to 'Fall in', in 'column of route' – but facing the rear. The 'Quick March' saw the troops returning to reoccupy

---

4 This reference to the 1914 'Retreat from Mons' by the British Expeditionary Force was likely to appeal to those readers of *The Old Contemptible* magazine who, as surviving members of the 'contemptible little army' (as the Kaiser had allegedly termed it), had participated in the action. Chaplain Bickersteth was also with an army detachment approaching Mons and made the same comment about the British returning to where they began (*Bickersteth* JB, p. 296).
5 11 November 1918 – 'the eleventh hour of the eleventh day of the eleventh month'.

the billets they had vacated only a few hours before. This was an unwelcome move, and a slump in the men's spirits set in, for it brought to an end what had been the most exhilarating part of the campaign – their irresistible advance.

Considerable freedom was allowed the troops that evening, although there was little to offer them in the semi-deserted village. A few decided to share with the civilians the evensong service in the church, but scarcely a soul became vocal, and many quietly wept, the atmosphere being moving and emotional.

That night sleep tarried. Many of the Tommies appointed themselves auxiliary advisers to the War Office, recommending to the Minister of War what should happen in the new circumstances. He might have been interested in the brisk suggestions that were offered in order to make his task easy, at least at that stage. It was well into the night when the voice of a Tommy groaned: 'Well, I'm .... Old Fritz has beaten us at the last fence, after all. The devils! And we are to be robbed of giving him a taste of what he deserves!' How true it was. He had so skilfully planned his surrender as to avoid disaster both to himself and his country. Instead of Berlin, our destination was to be only the banks of the Rhine.[6]

Some relief came when, on parade next morning on the village market-patch, a proud and cheery Brigade Commander addressed the men, congratulating them on the splendid way they had behaved during the whole 'show' and thus brought about such a great victory. A few scarcely approving gestures and grunts were the only signs that the men had registered his commendation of them. 'Men, let me say this one thing. An Army's honour does not depend only on its work in the field of action but on its behaviour in the hour of victory. Even a beaten army claims the conqueror's consideration.' Within a few minutes from the dismissal, almost every Tommy produced from his kitbag the material for polishing buttons and cleaning boots. And he whistled away, among the general and habitual grouses about such an occupation.

---

6 Arguably, the Tommies were right. The war ended without any of the Allied forces (other than prisoners of war) on German soil, a feature which helped to give rise to the myth that the German army was never defeated but was betrayed by the politicians in Berlin, a notion that eventually encouraged German bellicosity under Hitler and helped bring about World War II.

Epilogue

Looking Back

The adaptation of the Army machine to the new conditions of Armistice was almost as difficult a task as any other in the war, but the inevitable and welcome improvement all round soon became noticeable. The times of hardship, peril and the uncertainty of actual conflict gave place to the comforts and security of the semi-peace that followed the Armistice. Soon the ministries of religion began to assume more of their official guise and there was the possibility of the restored 'parade service' dwarfing, but perhaps actually spoiling, the more practical work of the past two years.[1] There was the temptation also to imagine that there would be but little call upon the ministries of consolation and help now that actual risk and suffering were eliminated, yet each phase of the war had its own peculiar temptations and dangers. The preventive grace and staying powers necessary for personal religion were more than ever needed in the perilous days of success, especially for the victors in the land of the vanquished.

While the Staff at G.H.Q. were busy drafting terms of peace and working out details of their plans for demobilisation, considerable new responsibility was thrown upon the Chaplains' Department. The many extra hours of leisure which came to the troops had to be filled with varied and interesting pastimes to counteract the dangers of an idle mind and idle hands.[2] Talks and lectures on subjects of topical and national interest, and especially propaganda work for the War Office, that of explaining the plans for demobilisation, were the supplementary tasks allotted to the

---

1 That is, Rider's two years as a chaplain.
2 Perhaps one of the dangers to the mind was felt to be that of ingesting the 'Bolshevik' propaganda which was having some effect across western and central Europe. In late November 1918 Chaplain Bickersteth noted that 'the Army is waking up to the fact that the man has a soul, or at least a mind, and we are being inundated with educational and recreational schemes' (*Bickersteth* JB, p. 302).

Chaplains. However, students of history felt somewhat hesitant about painting in too alluring colours the anticipated Utopia which the Authorities presumed would follow the signing of the Peace Treaty. The 'Notes' supplied by the Authorities seemed to suggest that those responsible for them had either forgotten or ignored the lessons from the past. No allowance was made for the inevitable 'back-wash' that had always followed as the unhappy sequel to such massive upheavals.

The days of Armistice were to be the real testing time for the men, for they had yet to face up to new and more luring personal temptations. Those remaining in France and Belgium found themselves with little to do in an hospitable country, amid a grateful populace. They were allowed to mix freely with the members of both sexes, and there was an intimacy to which the average Englishman was wholly unused, even on the highdays and holidays in his own country. This meant that new qualities of character were required to weather that particular moral storm. In military circles it was taken for granted that a reaction from war repressions and control would be inevitable, and steps were taken which did not help the men to face it heroically. Moral looseness was assumed, and instead of a firm discountenancing of it, was dealt with by those measures which allowed the sin in the belief that the full consequences of it could be prevented.[3] The work of the Chaplains was made infinitely more difficult by this semi-condoning attitude on the part of the Medical Authorities, for the men were inclined to regard any counsel given by Padres as mere ecclesiastical prudishness or a lack of understanding of human nature. How the plan worked out soon became apparent, and the Padre was involved to a greater extent than he had anticipated.

His last appointment was to a large French hospital, where, during the war, a glorious ministry of healing had been carried on in nursing back to health and strength those men who had met with misfortune 'in action'. Now his work there was less agreeable, for the patients were men who were suffering from venereal diseases which affected both body and soul. Here and there could be found an instance where a man was callous enough to treat his condition with indifference, but in the vast majority of cases there was a feeling of shame that pronounced its own judgement on what had happened. That wonderful buoyancy of spirit so common in the ordinary hospitals where the Tommies were nursed, the product of at least a healthy outlook upon life and its duties, was almost entirely absent

---

3   For the issuing of condoms to the troops, and access to licensed brothels, see note 55 of the Introduction.

from this hospital, and this placed a tremendous handicap upon anything attempted in the nature of pastoral visitation.

The closing chapter in the life of the Padre overseas was the least happy one. In the 'confidence' given to him by men who came under his care, he saw how much of the good that the actual fighting had brought out in them had been undone by the thoughtless actions of the days of peace. The home life and family associations for which men had risked their lives had been invaded through the back door by a foe whose presence it was impossible to conceal, and by a mistrust that was as dangerous as any enemy dressed in the field grey of the Central Powers. Such was the last element of real parson's work he was called upon to do overseas. But his work was to be continued in the Homeland soon after, for demobilisation did not dismiss him from the service in which he had been engaged.

A re-adjustment had to be made, so he was glad of the few days respite before taking up the work in a real church of his own, where he would be delivered from all those restrictions upon his usefulness imposed by rank and the regulations of the military machine.[4] He tried in those days to register the gains of the past five interminable years spent with his fellows in circumstances which he had never dreamt would have to be a part of his education. At least, he thought, he could claim that he knew men pretty thoroughly, so much so that he might have to use his knowledge to warn his colleagues in the home church that they were inclined to misjudge others and misinterpret their individual actions. No longer could he regard the Prophet Jeremiah as an authority on human nature, when all he could say about his fellows was that 'the heart of man was deceitful above all things and desperately wicked',[5] for experience had taught him that either Jeremiah had had very different material to judge from or else that he had failed to assess its inherent value. On his retirement as a Padre, he was greatly encouraged by the thought that in his home church he would have the same personnel to work with, and that they would bring with them a splendid new spirit of loyalty and devotion.

Another lesson he had learnt – one to which fact he attributed most of the smoothness with which he had been able to carry on his work as a chaplain – was that it was necessary to separate essentials from unessentials in the Christian life. Such things as denominational rights were unimportant, and apart from the fact that one had to register oneself as

---

4 After the war, Rider worked at first in the Wimborne (Hampshire) Methodist circuit, but thereafter mainly in Lancashire.
5 Jeremiah 17:9.

belonging to one or other of the 'persuasions', there was only one Church, and that Universal. He recognised, however, that the Roman Church had enjoyed many advantages during the campaign. The war had been fought in countries where 'Roman Catholic' was the state religion.[6] The general populace was of that faith; most villages had, at both entries, the sacred figure of the Crucifix, as well as a common public shrine inviting men's religious courtesies; and the village church with its resident priest and in many cases its general ecclesiastical equipment was at the service of Roman Catholic troops. Nevertheless, the shared Christian heritage could be claimed as common property by all who sought any ministry, and in that respect it was a constant reminder to men of all classes and creeds that the Christian religion was part and parcel of the social life of any British community.

It was therefore with high hopes that the one-time Padre set about his new job. He intended, first of all, to marshal for the work of his church men's rediscovered spirit of loyalty, their allegiance to the Cause of Righteousness, and the invincible courage which had showed itself when men were up against odds. He left a place in his church affairs and offices for his old pals, whom he felt sure would be able to illustrate practical Christianity in a form somewhat new to his more self-satisfied parishioners. Soon would the latter have the privilege of the co-operation of men who were willing, at any cost, to answer a call of need; men who had practised unselfishness in times both of want and of plenty; men who had been courageous in battle, heroic in pain, calm in dangers that regularly threatened their lives; men who had learned to recognise the voice of God in their sense of duty to one another, and who had shown a wonderful readiness to obey it; finally, men who knew their fellows, even their enemies, well enough to be able to love them, and to hate the means whereby fellow men had been exterminated.

But he waited many months. At first he excused the men for their delay on the grounds of their need of absolute rest and change. Occasionally he had the joy of grasping the hand of an old comrade who dropped into a service to see him. But he soon realised that he was going to be left alone in his job. Yet certain he was, that the men could not have become suddenly irreligious, and that the Cause for which they had fought must still have their sympathy. The ministries which they had previously accepted so gladly, and which he as a minister was still dispensing to his congrega-

---

6 Incorrect. But the leading and most influential Christian body in France and Belgium was the Roman Catholic church.

tion, seemed to suffer when they had to pass through the medium of a Church, and men showed no desire for them. He felt that while he had been taught to understand men better, he had failed to teach them to understand him or his work in the Church. He was baffled when he tried to explain why men could not find their natural place in the Church life, an experience all ministers will share with him until men who now hold aloof are willing honestly to state their reasons for so doing. There is, frankly, still some misunderstanding that keeps the Christian Church from the community it is most anxious to serve. We perhaps might ask ourselves whether the communal life of Army days did not introduce men to a life of comradeship, sacrifice and service that surpasses the fellowship of the average Christian society, where its truest expression is cramped by the introduction of a new set of rules and regulations imposed by another Headquarters' Staff.[7]

Today we are engaged in the same war as was waged in Europe during the years 1914 to 1918. Terrible though that phase of it was, it was but an incident in the age-long struggle of right against wrong. Each war in history has differed from the previous ones only in the kind of weapons used, these being fashioned according to the mode of the day in which the battle was being waged. Not until we learn the truth about the matter – that we 'fight not against flesh and blood but against principalities, against powers, against the world rulers of this darkness, against the spiritual hosts of wickedness in the heavenly places'[8] – shall we be likely to employ the weapons most suitable for the purpose. Each nation must empty its armouries of all save moral and spiritual forces if peace of the kind God would have his children know is to be enjoyed.

'Ruins advertise one's failures'. Allowing them to remain is bad policy. We must cover them up and begin to build again, this time a better structure. But for it, the same fine qualities which were found in men in the darker days of conflict will be necessary. England and the Church surely have a right still to hope that the men in whom these qualities of soul were brought to light in the long dark days of the Great War will throw in their lot with their old pals who still desire their support and comradeship. It is only the fact that God has a wonderful way of rescuing men from what would harm them, and using the very harms themselves to serve a nobler purpose, that makes any incident in a horrible war worth recording. To

---

7 A typical Nonconformist protest against the stifling of the 'free spirit' of individual Christian expression, usually directed against the set liturgies of the 'official churches'.
8 Ephesians 6:12.

some the War may have resulted in their moral degradation; happily, in the vast majority of cases, men learned more about the heights to which humanity can rise than about the depths to which it could sink.

'Man ... but a little lower than the angels'?[9]

---

9 Psalms 8:5.

Index

Armistice 137–40
Army Chaplains' Department 7, 75
army doctors 46, 108
Arras 39, 100–03

Bickersteth, Revd Julian 23, 35
1st Birmingham Pals Battalions (14th Warwickshire Regt) 3, 8, 25
    attack at High Wood 53–62
burials 104–05, 124–25

censoring letters 90–91
Church Parades 10, 34, 141
civilians 100–01, 128–30, 133–35
combat stress 72–73

Doundney, Revd Charles E. 23

ecumenism 144

gas attacks 92–95
German prisoners of war 109–13, 114–17, 135–36
ground attack aircraft 79–80, 87, 97–98

Handsworth Theological College 2, 6
horses 98–99, 131–32

Methodist Church's response to war 4–7
Methodist Times newspaper 28

mines 31–32, 38–44

Rider, Robert J.
    awarded Military Cross 33
    commissioned as a chaplain 74
    composition of memoirs 1, 21–23
    childhood and pre-WWI career 24
    ministering to the wounded 70, 120–21
    role as a chaplain 10–12, 14, 137
    views on soldiers 12–13
    views on war 15–16, 19–20
Roclincourt 41
Roman Catholic Church 144

Salvation Army 83–85
services 53–56, 78–79, 114–17
signalling 30, 41–42
soldiers' views on religion 53–54, 144–45
soldiers' views on war 52–53, 140

Tedstone, Lance-Corporal R.R. 65

Vaux-sur-Somme 49
venereal diseases 142–43

War Poets 17–18, 36,
Woods, Lieutenant 86–89, 93–94,
Watkins, Revd O.S. 27
World War II 145